Ever feel gritty? I do. I get gru..., resentful. Heidi McLaughlin says we're all a little bit sandy, in *Sand to Pearls*, she shows us that God doesn't want us to stay in the grittiness of life-consumed with the "what ifs", overpowered by the "should" and stuck in the past. He wants to transform us as we choose pearls over sand; healing over resentment; rejoicing over regret. Just the diagnosis for a rich, more beautiful life.

SHEILA WRAY GREGOIRE, speaker and author.
tolovehonorandvaccum.blogspot.com

Authentic. Practical. Powerful. *Sand to Pearls* is a resource guaranteed to encourage readers of God's desire and ability to transform our past into a promise-filled present and future. Thank you, Heidi, for sharing these wise words with us.

GRACE FOX, author of *Moving From Fear to Freedom*
and National Co-Director of International Messengers Canada.

I'm up to chapter five and loving it, I can't wait to read the whole thing. *Sand to Pearls* is chocked full of wisdom, practical, joy-filled and inspiring. Heidi scratches where women itch on subjects of friendship, over-commitment and being bound by our obligations to do more. This is a book you will not want to put down. Thank you for writing such a timely and important book for women today.

DEBBIE TAYLOR WILLIAMS, author of *The Plan A Woman in a Plan B World*,
speaker and Bible teacher.

Grounded in Scripture and the vulnerability of a sincere Christ follower, this book is a tool for women to savor and act upon. Reading Heidi McLaughlin's words will help women of faith to feel less alone on their journey toward wholeness.

NANCY BEACH, Champion for the Arts, Willow Creek Association, and Author of
Gifted to Lead. The Art of Leading as a Woman in the Church.

Sand
to Pearls

Making *BOLD* Choices
to Enrich Your Life

Heidi McLaughlin

Scripture quotations marked "NIV" are taken from the Life Application Bible, New International Version, Zondervan Publishers, copyright © 1988, 1989, 1990, 1991.

Scripture quotations marked "MSG" are taken from The Message. Copyright © by Eugene H. Peterson, 1993, 1994, 1995, 1996, 2000, 2001, 2002. Used by permission of NavPress Publishing Group.

Scripture quotations marked "NLT" are taken from the Holy Bible, New Living Translation, copyright © 1996. Used by permission of Tyndale House Publishers, Inc., Wheaton, Illinois, 60189. All rights reserved.

Scriptures marked "TLB" are taken from The Living Bible Paraphrase, Tyndale House Publishers, copyright © 1971, 1973.

Published by
Deep River Books
Sisters, Oregon
Deepriverbooks.com

Library of Congress Control Number: 2010940858

ISBN-10 1-935265-43-1
ISBN-13 978-1-935265-43-6

Cover and interior design by Robin Black, www.blackbirdcreative.biz

Heidi uses her passion and gifts of speaking and writing in her ministry called "HEART CONNECTIONS." You can contact her through her web page: www.heartconnection.ca or write to her at:

Heidi McLaughlin
1529 Chardonnay Place
West Kelowna, British Columbia
Canada V4T 2P9

To my pearls:
You evoke priceless laughter and adventure
simply by letting me be your Nana.
Always know that your choices have the power
to unleash your God-given dreams.

To my grandchildren:
Mya
Austin
Anthony
Matthew
Ryan
Cavan
Breanna
Alex
Brendon

To Laurie,

Thank you for taking the
"Pearl" journey.

Blessings,

Heidi McLaughlin

Contents

Acknowledgments

Writing a book starts with restlessness; a desire and passion that just won't go away. It feels like the irritation of a grain of sand that pokes, rubs and consumes my thoughts throughout the day and night. The first stimulation that keeps my heart pounding is believing that God has given me enough words, and that He will help me to fulfill my hopes and dreams of writing and completing another book. Then comes the real awakening; the reality of writing a book proposal, sending it to publishing houses and hoping and praying that someone will believe in me. When I sent my book proposal to Bill Carmichael, the founder of Deep River Books, he was bird hunting in Montana. He texted me from his iPhone to let me know he had received my proposal and that his editorial team would look at it in the coming weeks. As always, he was true to his word and I heard from him within the week. Deep River has been a huge, integral piece of my sand to pearl journey, not only because they agreed to publish this book, but because they are a company with a heart that honors God. Bill and his wife Nancie care about their authors; they believe in them and evoke courage in them to unleash their God-given stories. They treat all their authors with love, respect, and are always true to their words. Lacey Ogle, who leads the editorial team, works tirelessly and patiently to help authors craft a book that is sensitive to the author's passion and personality and lines up with God's leading.

Now come the people who help me transform my dreams into beautiful pearls. These are my priceless treasures God places in my life to spur me on and rub me the right way so that my uncultured words can be crafted into something valuable, inspiring and beautiful. As always, my husband Jack relentlessly reads every word that I have ever written. I trust and value his loving critiques and editing. He manages to help me see my stories from a different perspective by stepping back and taking the 10,000-foot view. His profound insights give me courage to let my words be authentic and truthful. He protects my time and helps me to stay in those quiet places where I can listen for God to give me new words.

My sister Brigitte is my faithful and gorgeous cheerleader. Not only was she my reader, she gave me indispensable viewpoints, encouragement and covered me with her love and prayers. Thanks also to my brother-in-law Bernie, who has incredible insight into details.

I am surrounded and blessed by my loving and supportive family. My son Donovan and daughter Michelle are the joy and delight of my life. They make it clear that they are proud of me, and their support transforms my courage into downright reckless boldness. My stepchildren, Janice, Jennifer and David encourage me every time we spend time together. My daughters-in-love Erika and Joanne are beautiful, energetic women who give me great insights into the need for making wise choices in this complicated life. I am very grateful to all my handsome sons-in-law, Tim, Mark and Ken. I delight in the way they raise their children and treat their wives. They are authentic, godly role models wherever they go. Each one of my children impacts my life in a unique and beautiful way.

There are many friends that pray for me, hold me accountable and give beneficial insight on my writing journey. Thank you for your sacrificial love and support.

Then finally, but mostly importantly, have been my mother's consistent and faith-filled prayers. Just knowing that my mother prays for me daily keeps me saturated and safe in God's love and plans for my life. Consequently this book is written as an act of worship and praise to God. God, my Creator, is the One who put the words in my heart, and He is the only One who can unleash them. I thank Him for giving me the passion to use my stories to help transform other people's lives—from sand to pearls.

Introduction

s I drive to work in the mornings, I gaze at people's faces and observe their fatigued, lifeless expressions as they navigate through traffic to confront another demanding day. Often I sit across a cup of coffee with another woman and I hear her sighs of feeling lonely and overwhelmed with too many obligations and choices. Life is tough these days and many people feel trapped. We grind through our days doing the same thing again and again and hope for different results. That could be described as the roadway to insanity. We don't know how to stop. We are on a relentless quest to know that we are loved, to know that we have value, and to feel pleasure. We will do almost anything to feel better.

We may have the illusion that:

- If I had a better career and worked harder, I would feel more fulfilled.
- When I have more money, life will be easier and I will feel more content.
- If I had a husband/boyfriend that treated me better, I would be a happier person.
- If I had had a better upbringing, I would have achieved greater success.
- My parents were overweight, poor and lazy; therefore, I will probably be like my parents.
- If I put my children into a lot of activities, I will feel like I am a good mother.
- If I had more time to myself, I would not be so tired.

And so we grab for the first thing that we think will make us happier; go and buy something we can't afford, pursue a different relationship, take another drink, open the fridge, watch some pornography, take a trip or sit on the couch and watch endless, boring television.

You and I are our own worst enemy, but we feel helpless to change. We need more than our human endeavors and wisdom to help us make choices to navigate this complicated maze of life. The Bible tells us that we have been given the mind of Christ, a supernatural authority, to unleash all the wisdom and discernment needed to make bold and good choices. Every single day God gives you and me the amazing privilege and power to choose a glorious course for our life. We can't even begin to imagine all the blessings God wants us to have and enjoy. "No eye has seen, no ear has heard, no mind has conceived what God has prepared for those who love him—but God has revealed it to us by his Spirit. The Spirit searches all things, even the deep things of God" (1 Cor. 2:9-10, NIV).

I am a perfect example of how God can take our worst decisions and biggest mistakes, and turn them into a magnificent new beginning. My spiritual journey did not start until I was thirty-two. I had been a rebellious, self-centered young woman determined to show my family and the world that I was capable of making my own wise choices. But my insecurities and selfishness propelled me to make choices that forged the pathway to a pit of depression, despair, tumultuous disappointments and "almost divorce." God, in His kindness, gently taught me how to begin to live a new life evoked by choices through the power of His Holy Spirit living in me.

Few things in life create more worry, stress and anxiety than the uncertainty of our future. While you are reading this book, it doesn't matter what stage of life you are at. God has the potential to use everything in your life, the good and bad, and turn it into beauty. It's time to choose and live your dream; but what tomorrow holds is up to you.

I would like you to imagine sitting across from me, sharing a delicious, hot steaming drink, being honest and making ourselves vulnerable. You need to know you are not alone in your daily toil. By being authentic we can soften our hearts and enable God to connect with us so that we can hear Him speak His truth and wisdom to us. Every chapter in this book begins with my own struggles, mistakes and challenges, and then gives insight as to why and how we make our destructive choices. Of course I don't leave you hanging and bleeding; I give you a dozen or so practical steps to empower you to make wise, bold choices that will enrich and transform your life in more beautiful ways than you can imagine. Then I end with a time of reflection and prayer. This is the place where you can allow the Holy Spirit, through the mind of Christ in you, to change your life from irritating sand into gorgeous, timeless pure pearls:

Stop and Ask God To Help You Change Sand to Pearls
Begin by asking: Ask God a question.

S: Scripture verse. A verse will be available here for reflection.

T: Thanksgiving. Thank God for what He has the power to accomplish.

O: Observation. What wisdom is God unleashing for you in this verse?

P: Prayer. Ask Him. I will end each chapter praying with you because I am passionate about God transforming everything in your life into what He created you to be. I may never have met you, but I have encountered women like you for the past twenty-five years and I have witnessed God's transforming power, changing struggles to joy—sand to pearls. I know He can because He is the King of kings and Lord of lords, Creator of all life—including yours. It's time to make choices that will forge the pathway God has planned for you. It's time to live your dream.

Chapter 1

Obligation or Invigoration

Is That a "Should" on Your Shoulder?

> *Our obligation is to give meaning to life and*
> *in doing so to overcome the passive, indifferent life.*
>
> —ELIE WIESEL, American Novelist

My fingers were slippery and sweaty, yet felt ice cold and numb. It was impossible to find the right chords on my guitar. My heart was pounding so loudly that I couldn't hear my own voice as I tried to sing the first verse of Moses and Miriam's victory song: that festive, praise-filled epic poem about the Israelites crossing the Red Sea. I took a deep breath, took a sip of water and tried again: "I will sing to the Lord for he is highly exalted, the horse and its rider he has hurled into the sea" (Exod. 15:1, NIV).

It was no use trying to sing a victorious song when I was the one feeling like I was being hurled into a sea of resistance. My face was burning with humiliation as I desperately tried to salvage this disaster, but I couldn't find my voice. As I glanced at the circle of women around the room, I could tell by their faces that I had failed miserably. My song was only half-finished, but I knew it was over. As I walked out of the room, a younger woman walked beside me and sweetly chirped, "Maybe God is trying to teach you something about your pride." Now I felt like I had been hit in the stomach by a sharp-edged rock. It took my breath away. I couldn't even answer her and walked out of the church vowing I would never go back in there again.

Just weeks before, some of my new church friends had approached me and said, "Heidi, I hear that you play the guitar and sing; we would love it if you would come to our next ladies event and bless us with your music." I had agreed to sing for these ladies, even though I knew I wasn't qualified. In spite of my misgivings, I still felt obligated to follow through on my commitment. People had spurred me on to do it. "You really should do it, you really should at least try," they had said. While uncertain of my singing and guitar playing, my sense of inferiority overpowered me and I was too intimidated to say no.

Yet I wanted to feel like I belonged to this group of Christian women that seemed so confident and gifted in many ways. This was in the early 1980s when I first became a Christian and desperately wanted to fit in—to be like one of them. With this harsh reality of being humiliated in front of my peers, I discovered that singing and playing the guitar was not one of the gifts God had given me.

When we feel overpowered by people or our circumstances, it provokes our feelings of inferiority. It unleashes confusion, frustration, and we short-circuit the gifts, purpose and joy God has prepared for us. We wear ourselves out pleasing people instead of God, and by doing so we deny Christ's power in our life because we are afraid of what people will think of us. When Jesus ascended from this earth, He left us the Holy Spirit; He gave us the "mind of Christ" (1 Cor. 2:16, NIV), and passed on to us His authority. Instead we struggle through life reacting to all the "shoulds" that life heaps on us, and we end up with our shoulders hunched over looking like we are carrying the weight of the world. Trying to please everyone is very exhausting; it drains us of energy and unknowingly we succumb to the authority of other people instead of Christ. The faster we go and the harder we work at trying to juggle all our responsibilities, the emptier we feel.

Marcus Buckingham, the author of *Find Your Strongest Life*, says this about the *shoulds*. "Because you neglect the specific moments that strengthen you, your life gradually becomes filled up with a grab bag of activities and responsibilities. You may have a good reason for taking on each of these responsibilities—everything from 'If I don't do this, no one else will' to 'A good mother *should* do this' but the outcome is that a barrage of moments with which you've filled your life now blankets your senses. This barrage drowns out the signals from those few moments that truly strengthen you. You start to feel empty."[1]

When we operate out of our weaknesses and lack of self-worth, the slightest demands have the power to intimidate us. The word "intimidate" is an active verb that has a very negative connotation. The thesaurus describes it this way: "threaten, badger, bait, bluster, bully, coerce, constrain, cow, dispirit, subdue," and so on.[2] When we submit to these destructive words, we refute all that we have been created for, and deny the gifts and power God wants to unleash in us. God never bullies us. Instead, He wants to take an active part in our life and is interested in everything we do and who we are. Look at how He values us: "What's the price of two or three pet canaries? Some loose change, right? But God never overlooks a single one. And he pays even greater attention to you, down to the last detail—even numbering the hairs on your head! So don't be intimidated by all this bully talk. You're worth more than a million canaries" (Luke 12:6-7, MSG).

Don't be intimidated by bully talk. It's hard for women to get up each morning and try to compare their worth against a million canaries. When they look in the mirror they can't imagine that anyone is interested in their hair. Dr. Dobson says that the biggest struggle for women is their low self-esteem, so it is much easier to try to listen and cave in to the bully talk and earn approval by simply giving in to other people's expectations. We need to be able to separate the bully talk and guilt induced *shoulds* that we are caving into. Let's look at some of the real obligations we do need to attend to every day. We should:

- Brush our teeth.
- Eat healthy foods.
- Pay our bills on time.

- Wash our clothes.
- Show up at work on time.
- Treat each other with love and respect.
- Work on our marriages and relationships.
- Forgive.
- Love the Lord our God with our all heart, soul and mind, and our neighbor as ourselves.

We should do all those things that promote our physical, emotional and spiritual health. How do we know when these have turned into obligations that stagnate our soul?

My friend, Beth Hanishewski, who is a life coach, describes it this way: "I have done many things out of obligations. The funny thing is, it does not matter if it was an invitation, a plan, a favor, gift, solicitation or a guilt trip attempt. All of these situations had one thing in common—a heavy energy. The energy of obligation feels constricting and it creates anxiety and fear. I try to override these emotions in order to please someone, or worse, to look good."[3]

So how do we define what we *should* do?

What Is That "Should" on Your Shoulder?

While I am writing this book I am also facilitating a study called *One Month to Live: Thirty Days to a No-Regrets Life*, written by Kerry and Chris Shook. On our group's first evening together, one of the questions was, "What is one thing you would stop in your life right now if you knew you only had thirty days to live?" After a lively discussion, one main theme began to come into focus; *stopping the life-sucking "shoulds" out of our daily activities.* They are the guilt-induced obligations that we do because we are afraid that people might not like us. The discussion got even livelier as we tried to determine the obligations that we needed to let go. How do we know the difference between what to hold and what to fold?

Here is what I ask myself: "If intimidation discourages me from using the gifts God has given me, makes me feel obligated to give in to people's demands and robs me of energy; then what wakes me up and makes me feel alive, bold and passionate? How can I use my God-given gifts to make daily impacts in people's lives?" Here is where I need to look at the source of my moment-by-moment power.

1. Self-Power Induces Obligation

The story of Ananias and Sapphira is a great example of how deceptive and sneaky we can become when we acquiesce and do things out of obligation and needing people's approval. In the early church in the book of Acts, at a time when all believers were of one heart and mind, people were asked to sell their houses and land and give the money to the apostles to give to others in need. Ananias and Sapphira wanted to be a part of this great plan, probably to have people look favorably on them for their generosity. So they sold some property but deceived the church by holding back part of the money. They were caught and Peter confronted them. He said, "Ananias, why have you let Satan fill your heart? You lied to the Holy Spirit, and you kept some of the money for yourself. The property was yours to sell or not sell, as you wished. And after selling it, the money was also yours to give away. How could you do a thing like this? You weren't lying to us but to God" (Acts 5:3-4, NLT).

We are especially weak when it comes to covering our hide and protecting our image. Who doesn't want people to admire them, praise them for generosity or some noble deed? Sometimes we are afraid that if we don't go along with the crowd, people won't like us, we won't fit it; and we concede to self-power. If we constantly operate out of our self-power, we will feel defeated by the constant demands of choices that we must make in our daily activities. A high percentage of women are finding it difficult to cope with the demands and choices they have to make in this exhausting twenty-first-century life, and cope by being on anti-depressants or other mind-altering drugs to give them the tenacity to carry on.

Marcus Buckingham in his book, *Find Your Strongest Life*, tells us that succumbing to busyness and doing more does not make us happy. "Over the last forty years women have secured for themselves greater opportunity, greater achievement, greater influence and more money. But over the same time period, they have become less happy, more anxious and more stressed; and in ever-increasing numbers they are medicating themselves for it."[4]

To save our soul, you and I have to be brutally intentional about learning how to make choices by operating through God's power.

2. God's Power-Passion Invigorates

I get passionate and excited when I see men and women who are bold, relentless and wide awake to pursue the passions, gifts and abilities God has given them. Kerry and Chris Shook tell us in their book, *One Month to Live*: "We're created as spiritual beings, and to develop spiritual energy, we have to cultivate a healthy connection to our Creator. The Bible consistently reveals that humans are created in God's image and that we have an eternal part of us, our spirits. The most important part of our lives is our spiritual dimension, our souls… we're created to be connected to a larger power source."[5]

How do we know we are living an invigorated, passionate life that is connected to a larger power? Look at the luscious fruit.

I love living in the beautiful Okanagan Valley, the heart of British Columbia. I never get tired of looking out of our kitchen window and watching the activity in the vineyards. For the past thirteen years I have been walking through these vineyards at least twice a week. In the last month I watched the vineyard workers carefully cut the lush, sweet grapes from the vines. Today my husband and I noticed that all the grapes are gone, and most of the vines have had their leaves stripped by the recent autumn winds. I also know that after the winter season is done, there will be more workers in the fields with their pruning shears trimming the vine branches back to almost nothing. Even after all these years I am amazed how the pruners remove all but the two best side shoots that grow from the stem. Over the next few months I watch how these harshly pruned branches begin to produce lush, sweet grapes. If you and I are going to bear gorgeous fruit in our lives, we have to be connected to the source of that growth. I love the way these verses explain this process:

> "I am the true vine, and my Father is the gardener. He cuts off every branch in me that bears no fruit, while every branch that does bear fruit he prunes so that it will be even more fruitful. You are already clean because of the word I have spoken to you. Remain in me, and I will remain in you. No branch can bear fruit by itself; it must remain in the vine. Neither can you bear fruit unless you remain in me. I am the vine; you are the branches. If a man remains in me and I in him, he will bear much fruit; apart from me you can do nothing" (John 15:1-5, NIV).

To make this power work in our life we have to pay attention to four things:

i. We have to stay attached to the vine, because it is the life source for growing the fruit. We need to be saturated by the word of God because that is the source of all our wisdom and strength, and it speaks to the mind of Christ that is within us.

ii. Without being attached to the vine, "we can do nothing." Sure, we can be involved in a lot of activities and succumb to all the "shoulds"; but what are we accomplishing that will have eternal value?

iii. We need to be pruned regularly of our criticism, self-righteousness and immoral life so that we can continue to grow to be kinder, more compassionate, extending forgiveness and becoming more like Christ.

iv. God cuts off any branch that does not bear fruit. Ouch! I don't really want to know what that means.

When we choose to tap into the power of God's truth about who we are and what He can accomplish through us, it will illuminate our strengths and evoke passion. Soon a great transition begins to take place in our lives.

We move from "I should" to "I get to." When we are passionate about something, watch out: ridiculous things begin to happen.

Change the "Shoulds" to "Ridiculous Risks"

Operating out of our God-given strengths makes us confident, passionate and bold enough to say no to the world's screaming demands and to say yes to take some ridiculous Kingdom risks. Here is how John Bevere in his book, *Breaking Intimidation*, describes boldness: "Boldness comes from the virtues of power, love and soundness of mind. Boldness is not a virtue in itself. We have all known people who were brazen and bold. True boldness comes from God and is fueled by godly virtue. Boldness that is fueled by God's character awakens the gifts in our lives."[6]

Two of my favorite stories that encourage me in ridiculous boldness are of a soon-to-be king and a queen.

1. When we think of David the shepherd boy, we think of king, but also of giant killer. King Saul tried to caution David about killing a giant. "'Don't be ridiculous!' Saul replied. 'There's no way you can fight this Philistine and possibly win. You're only a boy'" (1 Sam. 17:33, NLT). But the size of the giant was not enough to block the view of God for this young boy when he took out his five smooth stones. He had ridiculous courage because he knew, "And everyone assembled here will know that the Lord rescues his people, but not with sword and spear. This is the Lord's battle, and he will give you to us!" (1 Sam. 17:47, NLT). David's source of ridiculous power was in knowing that God ultimately fights all our battles.

2. Esther, the beautiful young Jewish woman that stole a king's heart, is the stunning main character in one of those "sitting on the edge of your seat" intrigue and romance stories that should be made into a Steven Spielberg movie. It's what fairy tales are made of—until a sinister plot is discovered. Queen Esther's cousin Mordecai discovered that there was an evil man named Haman who had drawn up

a letter that decreed all the Jews to be killed in that land. The dispatches said, "to destroy, kill and annihilate all of the Jews—young and old, women and little children—on a single day" (Esther 3:13, NIV). Queen Esther was also a Jewess, but how could she help? Even though she was a queen she could not approach the king without being summoned; she could be put to death.

Next come three powerful factors that fuel invigoration.

i. Her cousin Mordecai reminded Queen Esther of her destiny. These people that were going to be killed were *her people, her family.* He reminded her how God uses us to accomplish His Kingdom work on earth when he said, "And who knows but that you have come to royal position for *such a time as this?*" (Esther 4:14, NIV, italics mine). This powerful reminder shows us that we need to be crystal clear about our purpose and set our priorities, so that we can take action and move boldly ahead.

ii. Even though Esther was a queen and shared the king's wealth and power, she still needed God's power. It is foolish to think that human wealth or position can make us impervious to danger. Queen Esther then replied to Mordecai, "Go, gather together all the Jews who are in Susa, and fast for me. Do not eat or drink for three days, night or day" (Esther 4:15-16, NIV). By calling for a fast, Queen Esther was demonstrating that she knew she needed God's power to be ridiculously bold on this dangerous mission.

iii. The world's motto is "save your skin and look out for number one," but we need to decide what God wants us to accomplish on this earth and trust Him for the boldness to do it. Queen Esther knew she was laying her life on the line for this treacherous mission. Her words, "And if I perish, I perish" (Esther 4:16, NIV) send a shiver through my spine. Queen Esther felt passionate about her purpose and mission, completely trusting God for the outcome that saved the lives of all the Jews in that country.

When I am reminded of my destiny; that I am a child of the Creator and He sent His Son to die for me and that He has a purpose for my life on this earth, at this time and place of all eternity, I can be ridiculously bold at times. Not Queen Esther style, but Heidi style:

- Traveling to Poland to teach on spiritual transformation. Only God could give me the boldness to do this.
- Speaking in Yellowknife, Yukon, and experiencing no washrooms or daylight for twenty-two hours of the day.
- Submitting manuscripts for publication. This required risk and trusting God would help me get them published.
- Asking my boss if I could reduce my work hours.
- Forgiving someone that hurt me deeply.

In order to find our own style of ridiculous boldness, we have to be clear about our purpose and priorities.

What To Keep and What To Throw Away

The Christmas season is one of the worst "should" occasions for women. For years I entered into this time of year with a love/hate relationship. The ambience in our home is enchanting when it is decorated with fresh evergreen, the room is filled with flickering candles and hundreds of white mini lights are strung on the tree and around the hearth. My family is my greatest external joy on this earth, and I cherish our times lingering by the fireplace, sipping a fragrant cider and listening to soft Christmas music.

But there are parts of the Christmas season that feel torturous and I approach them with disdain. For years I had a recurring nightmare wherein the stores were closing in one hour and I still hadn't started my Christmas shopping. Each time I woke up in a sweaty panic and realized how much there was still to do to finalize our family's Christmas preparations. Year after year it got more expensive and complicated, and by the time the Holy Christmas Eve arrived I was grumpy, exhausted and sometimes even sick.

Years ago I started to rebel against Christmas expectations and our family has truly been diligent about working with me to simplify the season's demands. We are all progressing; albeit slowly. In 2007, I chose to escalate the progress—significantly. I was so worn out with all the nonsensical "shoulds" of the season—all the expenses, the exhaustive decorating, shopping and wrapping—that Jack and I decided to cancel Christmas in our home that year. It was the perfect year to experiment with it because we were going to spend Christmas at my daughter's home in Alberta. I was shocked at how liberating it was not to decorate our home, send out cards or bake. I felt like a little kid that had just been let loose in a candy shop. Christmas demands, rituals and expectations were no longer going to make me feel obligated; and it absolutely invigorated me.

I shared my delightful discovery with many women and each time I told my story their eyes got big; then a smile broke out on their face and they laughed and cheered me on. Christmas 2009, we did it again. We celebrated Christmas at our daughter's home in Sacramento, where we spent our time walking, playing games, laughing and scouting out a great Christmas Eve service. The anticipation of being free from the Christmas expectations of outlandish spending, overeating and absurd money spent on wrapping paper and bows that end up in the garbage leaves me giddy with joy.

It's not an easy process to decide which "shoulds" we keep and which ones we throw away. I love my friend Beth's attitude and her method for determining her obligations:

"The first thing I do when I am asked to do anything is to check in with my body. How do I feel? Does this demand give me energy or deplete it? If, however, I am unsure and agree to this something, then I ask myself, 'Do I regret saying yes?' If that is the case, then there are only two choices left:

1. Go back and say no. (I may say something like this: 'I changed my mind. Forgive me for agreeing before I gave myself the time to think it through.')

2. Find a way to make it fun:
    a. Add music. (Even house cleaning can be improved with the right music.)
    b. Add intention. (What is the reward in this commitment?)
    c. Add a friend. (It is amazing how even the most arduous or tedious tasks can become fun with the right company.)

While the energy of obligation is heavy and un-fun, the hallmark of invigoration is energy."[7]

Steps to Finding Invigoration

Determining how to make our best choices each day is not determined by better time management or greater expertise in juggling our schedule. If you've ever watched a juggler, you will notice that his goal is to keep all the balls up in the air. That's what we do when we have a loaded, frantic lifestyle that drains the life out of us; we will constantly feel obligated and not invigorated. We don't give our best to anything; we do the least we can and then we're on to the next thing.

I believe there are a few other key factors in deciding what to do with the barrage of "shoulds":

1. Know the source of your power.
2. Know your purpose for this season of your life.
3. Prepare a mission statement (See Jack's and mine in Chapter 6). This is a very practical tool to determine what fits into your values and goals.
4. Ask very good questions.
    a. Does it fit into my life *"for such a time as this"*?
    b. What is my motive for doing this?
    c. What was my initial feeling when I was confronted with this task?
    d. Do I have the time?
    e. Will it take me away from valuable family commitments?
    f. Can I afford it?

    g. Is it in keeping with my strengths?

    h. Does it advance my learning and keep me interested?

    i. Does it energize me or deplete me?

5. Take the 10,000-foot view for some of the more complicated and challenging choices. We see things much clearer when we see life from a God angle.

    a. Will this matter six months or a year from now?

    b. Does it enhance my spiritual growth?

    c. Is it in keeping with my values?

    d. Is this part of God's plan for my life for doing his Kingdom work here on earth?

    e. Is this wasted time or is it a gift that God is trying to give me?

The invitation to sing and play my guitar left me with a negative sense of obligation to perform. The disaster that ultimately occurred left me humiliated and depleted, but it made me realize that this was not what God had gifted me for. For the next number of years it was frustrating for me to try and discover what I had been created to do. Most days it seemed that I didn't have a clue.

Through this tumultuous journey of trying to stay true to who God created me to be, I stayed connected to God and kept asking Him, "God, what are the gifts you have given to me so that I can make a significant difference in people's lives?" As God was preparing my bigger picture of being an author, speaker, teacher and mentor for women, I was content to do each day what God had prepared for me to do that day—love my family and love others. I learned that I needed the power of the Holy Spirit daily to give me the wisdom to separate my "shoulds" so that I could function not by feeling obligated, but by being invigorated.

Choices That Enrich Your Life

1. Realize that juggling your calendar or Blackberry is not the answer to an invigorated life. Choose to work out of values and priorities that strengthen and invigorate you.

2. Every day we have to make almost a hundred choices. Realize you can only do that day what God has prepared for that particular day. Choose to pray and give the day to God and let Him help you work it out.

3. Learn to discern between your people pleasing and God pleasing. Choose to dismiss the people pleasing and focus on what will bring value into your life and the people closest to you.

4. Sometimes we look at other people and think we will be happy and fulfilled when we do what they are doing. Choose to believe that God has made you unique and He has something different for you to do; your style, your way.

5. When you hear that you are worth more than a million canaries, do you believe how worthy you are to God? Choose to trust God that God is interested in every area of your life and that He will never take you any place where He will abandon you.

6. Have you been asked to do something ridiculous? Choose to see it through the 10,000-foot view instead of your immediate emotions.

7. You are at a time in your life where you think you should have figured out by now what God's purpose is for you. Choose to believe a) You may already be doing it and not even know it, or b) That God is preparing you for it.

8. Discover those things in your life that give you energy. You may not see them as gifts God has given you because they seem so effortless. Choose to believe that God can use those gifts to have a profound impact on this world.

9. You think you are handling life successfully because you are multitasking and keeping all your events in order. Choose to believe the fact that when you multitask your IQ drops by ten points and you are giving everything a divided attention.

10. You think that having more education, a better job, and better pay will make you feel more fulfilled. Choose to believe that those are all very good things to strive for, but they will never fully complete you and make you ultimately happier.

11. You believe this is your "lot in life" and there is nothing you can do about it. Choose to believe that you can break out of any pattern by learning to do things differently. Ask God to help you be creative.

12. Interruptions are part of life. Choose to believe that what frustrates you about them is that there is no margin in your life for these interruptions that may be disguised divine opportunities.

13. Choose to live each day by seeing life as a gift, and choose to see the good in everything and everyone. Choose joy.

Stop and Ask God To Help You Change Sand to Pearls

Begin by asking: God, what people-pleasing obligations deplete me?

S Scripture: "The fear of human opinion disables; trusting in God protects you from that" (Prov. 29:25, MSG).

T Thanksgiving: God I am so thankful that you will protect me and help me overcome the constant demands that this world places on me. Thank you that you have given me the wisdom and discernment through having the mind of Christ to know when I am caving in to obligations to please people instead of You.

O Observation: It is so important for me to feel loved and accepted. It is so true that I am afraid if I don't give in to the demands people place on me, I won't be accepted and liked.

P Prayer: God, I realize that You have given me twenty-four precious hours each day, and that each one of those is a gift to me. Help me to treat that gift with wisdom, love and a sound mind. I need to be reminded over and over again how much I am loved, how I have more worth than a million canaries, so that I can be empowered to make decisions out of a godly boldness. Help me each day to separate my "shoulds"—the ones that need to be done, and the ones that I need to throw away. Give me the wisdom to know the difference.

Thank You for all the opportunities You give me to make a difference on this earth. Help me never to miss any of those moments that may seem like an annoyance or interruption, but are in fact a gift that You are trying to give me.

Thank You that You are interested in all of me, and that You have a beautiful and powerful kingdom purpose for my life. God, please help me to see the world through eyes that are invigorated, not obligated.

Amen.

Chapter 2

Sabotage or Success

Breaking the "Nobody" Barrier

Everybody wants to be somebody; nobody wants to grow.
—JOHANN VAN GOETHE

We crave recognition. If you don't agree, rewind your mind to a time when you ran into a beloved old friend in a crowded room. Your eyes probably lit up with excitement when you met; you ran towards each other, hugged, then pulled back a little to check each other out and exchange flattering comments:

"It's so wonderful to see you again; you look so great."

"Wow, have you lost weight?"

"What have you done to your hair? It looks amazing."

"I don't know how you do it, but you haven't aged a day."

Did that make you feel recognized and valued? If you are still not sure, think back to a time when you received an award or a huge raise. How about the time your name appeared in the newspaper or someone sent you flowers for a special accomplishment? How did that make you feel? I am quite sure your face flushed with excitement, your heart pounded just a little bit faster, you felt adored and felt like a *somebody*.

All of us were created to be a *"somebody"* and when our worth is acknowledged we secretly feel we have been validated. From the time that we are little children, we want the world to notice us, to affirm our value and celebrate us. John Maxwell, an international author and speaker on leadership, acknowledged this fact in his book, *Dare to Dream...Then Do It*, in which he tells us that the number one thing he knows about people is that "Everybody wants to be Somebody."[8] After teaching and interacting with people for almost twenty-five years, I agree with him. Many women feel isolated and sad because no matter how hard they try, they feel like they are never good enough. They hardly ever feel like they belong. I often hear these words at retreats or conferences, "Heidi, everybody seems to belong, but I feel like a puzzle piece that just doesn't fit." Why do we feel this way—like a *nobody*?

In our hearts we know we were meant to be magnificent. The Bible puts it this way: "He has set eternity in the hearts of men" (Eccles. 3:11, NIV). We know there is more to life than we are experiencing. Occasionally we capture glimpses of a glorious, ideal life, yet when we look at ourselves in the mirror or at our circumstances, we see the harsh reality that isn't always pretty. Most days we feel haggard, overwhelmed, rushed, trying very hard to find a pair of matching earrings, socks or our car keys. We struggle with this daily tension between our perception of the ideal life and the present unsatisfying reality. Something happened to sabotage the ideal image of who we thought we would be and what our life would look like.

Designed, Not Defined

We are in a battle against a powerful, false belief system. It is a subconscious, deeply ingrained habit of seeing the world through a set of deficient lenses that were shaped for us from the time we were born. This false belief system was formed by our interpretation of external events and the influence of our parents, neighbors, siblings, teachers and other people that were part of our day-to-day activities.

I am the middle daughter in our family, and each one of us children interprets situations and events differently. If all three of us were given the challenge to find a way to free a woman from sexual slavery in India, one of us would probably anonymously donate money, another one would probably want to fly over there to meet with the people involved, and another one might start a fundraising project to release slaves. None of these are wrong or right—they are just different.

Unfortunately, we live in an imperfect world with sinful, defective people and the lenses through which we see the world are distorted. Our subconscious gets in the way and we continually act on those untrue beliefs. We may want to go to the gym, but somehow we never make it. We talk about applying for a certain job, but we don't believe we have what it takes to succeed. These false beliefs are so acutely ingrained in us that we are in this daily subconscious tug-of-war to make our mental false picture match our present reality.

The truth is that we have been defined by an imperfect world, but we are designed by a perfect God. To see the truth of our life the way we were designed to live, we have to break the barrier of our false belief system. We have to choose to stop believing the lies about ourselves, and start working with God to believe the truth of the life Jesus died for. Listen to these reassuring words: "The thief comes only to steal and kill and destroy; I have come that they may have life, and have it to the full" (John 10:10, NIV). God wants us to have a satiated, chock-full life. He has designed us to experience a fulfilling soul life: we must settle for nothing less.

Therefore We Sabotage Ourselves

Self-sabotage is a protective mechanism that fights to defend the beliefs and feelings and circumstances we have become accustomed to. It is our low self-worth, lack of confidence and sense of inferiority that thwarts our efforts to know and receive the fullness of life. The biggest obstacle to grabbing on to the inner fulfillment of life is that we are our own worst enemy. Our false belief system may say:

- I'm not smart enough—*therefore,* I will never get that degree or be able to teach that Bible study.

- I'm too old—*therefore*, I will never be asked to speak or get that coveted career.
- My parents were overweight, poor and lazy—*therefore*, I will probably be like my parents. I will always struggle, so why bother trying?
- I come from a family of alcoholics—*therefore*, I am destined to become one as well.
- No one can be trusted—*therefore*, what is the point of making close friendships?
- People always let me down or disappoint me—*therefore*, I will do it myself.
- I feel insecure, like I never quite measure up—*therefore*, I will try to do everything perfectly.

For the first thirty-five years of my life, without realizing it, I sabotaged the joy, freedom and harmonious relationships that God wanted me to enjoy. I viewed my life through the lenses that lied to me and said, *If you work hard and do everything perfectly, you will be loved and admired.*

What's so bad about working hard and trying to do things perfectly? Nothing, unless we are afraid that if we don't do things perfectly, we will be paralyzed with fear of failing and not feel loved.

I turned into a working machine and succeeded at anything that was put in front of me—I would settle for nothing less. As a wife and mother, I canned my own fruits and vegetables, baked bread, stayed up until 3:00 a.m. to sew my own clothes and some of my children's. I also had a career as an administrator of a law firm, and could do almost anything that anyone asked me to do. If I didn't know how to do it, I would figure it out and I would strive to do it perfectly. This may sound noble, but all this determined performing was a lethal weapon that was slowly killing my soul and never gave me any peace. My mind was always on the next thing that I needed to do, and then measuring my success when it was completed. Perfectionism leaves no one out of the equation. I transferred some of those horrible high expectations and standards onto my husband

and children to make sure they fit into my perfect plans. Expectations are a disappointment just waiting to happen, because people weren't put on this earth to cater to our insatiable needs and to make us happy. A perfectionist is ugly to live with, because enough is never enough. Instead of laughter and joy, there is tension, anger and dissatisfaction when results and goals are not achieved.

I was dancing as fast as I could to please everyone, and in the relentless process I was losing my own soul. God must have seen how I was sabotaging the life flow of the work of the Holy Spirit and had me take a stark look in my soul mirror. Absolute fatigue and frustration brought me to a "Heidi meltdown." It felt like the whole world was working against me to make me miserable, and nothing seemed perfect enough for my satisfaction.

When we have a toothache, we run to a dentist; when we break a bone, we go to the hospital. When we realize our soul is wounded or broken, we need to run to the One who created us and knows us inside out. I cried, "God help me!" I know that God is always ready and waiting for us to come to this life-changing intersection. For the first time in my life I allowed myself to look in my mirror through God's eyes to see how I was trying to earn love by trying to be perfect. It was a shocking revelation to see the hideous reality that I was sabotaging my joy and peace by trying to earn the right to be a *somebody*—by trying to be perfect. How foolish, unrealistic and a waste of valuable time to expend time and energy on "stuff" that ultimately didn't matter. That event exposed the lies of my false belief system, which said that I needed to be perfect in order to be a *somebody*. I learned to agree with Liz Curtis Higgs in her grace-filled book *Embrace Grace*, "Striving for perfection can be exhausting, especially when you keep failing at it…. Perfectionism is all about me-me-me getting it right, and then being proud of myself for doing so (and judging others who aren't perfect). Groan."[9]

Over the next several years, I had to choose to learn that I deserved to be just who I was; that God loved me the way He created me. I had to learn to love myself that same way.

"Buts" and "What Ifs"

How tragic that a three-letter word has the power to sabotage so much of the goodness and blessing that God wants to pour out on our lives. God has been trying to save us from slavery from the beginning of time, *but* we just don't listen.

The Drive-In Movie Theatre in Prince George leaves a lasting memory etched in my mind. I can still see Charles Heston as Moses with his rod, handsome face and flowing robes in the *Ten Commandments* approaching Pharaoh and telling the king to "Let God's people go!"

From the beginning of creation, God has always wanted to save us from bondage—from things, or from ourselves. The exodus of the two million Israelites from Egypt to Kadesh-Barnea is one of the most dramatic Bible stories about God saving us from slavery. God used Moses to fulfill a promise that all these people would be released from bondage and get to live in Canaan, the Promised Land; an abundant land flowing with milk and honey.

After almost two years of wandering in the desert, they finally arrived at their long-awaited destination. Can you imagine how exciting this would have been? After all the hardships of walking through the hot, dusty, windy desert, wearing the same shoes, and longing for a soft bed and the comforts of home, they finally arrived. As they camped at the edge of the Jordan River, Moses picked twelve of his strongest, sharpest and smartest leaders and told them to go and check out the land. After forty days, these savvy guys returned and here is what they said: "We entered the land you sent us to explore, and it is indeed a bountiful country—a land flowing with milk and honey. Here is the kind of fruit it produces. *But* the people living there are powerful, and their towns are large and fortified" (Num. 13:27-28, NLT, italics mine).That small, insignificant three letter word "but" had the power to change everything.

It is heartbreaking for me to try to visualize this. The majority of the spies stood on the brink of the Promised Land; their eyes still on the land flowing with milk and honey. In one hand they were holding proof of God's promise, the gorgeous lush grapes, *but* on the other hand they did not have the courage to go in.

These people had been walking with God in the wilderness for almost two years; they saw God provide manna for them every day, watched water pour from a rock and witnessed and experienced the parting of the Red Sea. They had seen God provide protection and cool air during the day through a cloud, and fire gave warmth during the chilly nights in the desert. They had actually heard His voice at Mount Sinai, *but* ten out of the twelve spies still didn't trust or believe that God would help them overcome the powerful people in the land. Because they did not trust God to protect them and provide for them in the Promised Land, He left them to wander in the wilderness for another thirty-eight years.

However, the *but* doesn't stop there. Now we're into the *what ifs.*

Part of our sabotage plan is that we create our own mythical obstacles as to why we should not receive what God has promised. In the book *Joshua*, Phillip Keller gives the stages od what I believe is the sabotage to our promised, fulfilled life.

1. Facts—always look unbeatable and discouraging.
2. Fear—implanted by the enemy.
3. Fantasy—of foreboding, creating a "what if" scenario.
4. Failure—refusal to carry out God's plan.[10]

The *what ifs* had the people awake all that night, weeping, wailing and lamenting. "'If only we had died in Egypt, or even here in this wilderness!' they complained. 'Why is the Lord taking us to this country only to have us die in battle? Our wives and our little ones will be carried off as plunder! Wouldn't it be better for us to return to Egypt?'" (Num. 14: 2-3, NLT). Their doubting took their eyes off God's promises in order to create their own illusion of unbeatable obstacles.

I shake my head in despair every time I read these *what ifs.* What if we are missing out on promises that God has for us, simply because we don't have the confidence or courage to overcome the obstacles and go after them?

Many of us, when faced with a challenge or opportunity, are consumed with the mythical challenge instead of the goal. We settle for less. We wander around the same mountain year after year because the mountain blocks the view of our loving God who is just waiting to set us free.

In the study guide, *"One in a Million"* author Priscilla Shirer tells us about an enemy that is sabotaging us from receiving God's promises:

> "As you begin to feel a divine tugging in your heart and explore spiritual abundance by opening your ears to God's voice and looking for the manifested presence of God around you be sure you will draw the Enemy's attention. The Devil will not wait patiently for you to acquire your God-given inheritance. He knows that once you enter the abundant life of Canaan you will never want to leave. His goal is to scare you off before your palate can grow accustomed to the taste of milk and honey. With this in mind, we must adopt God's encouragement to Joshua. Sister, the task of taking Canaan is upon us. Now is the time to move forward without fear."[11]

There is milk and honey waiting for all of us, *but* what will it take to stop our self-sabotage and receive it?

Breaking Barriers

We need to start by choosing to break the barriers of our false belief system. This includes obliterating the negative self-talk that is a pack of lies from an enemy who does not want us to enjoy God's promises for a fulfilling, joyful life. Breaking any barrier is hard work, but the results are beyond anything you and I can dream or imagine. God has so much for us that He wants to reveal through the Holy Spirit that has been given to us. Listen: "No eye has seen, no ear has heard, and no mind has imagined what God has prepared for those who love him. But it was to us that God revealed these things by his Spirit. For his Spirit searches out everything and shows us God's deep secrets" (1 Cor. 2:9-10, NLT). I believe we will spend the rest of our lives breaking through our self-imposed sabotages to discover the unlimited resources God wants to reveal to us.

Let's begin to break the barriers of sabotage along the same lines that an airplane broke the barrier of sound—the explosion of a powerful breakthrough.

Sound travels at 1,236 kilometers or 768 miles per hour, or about one kilometer in three seconds and about one mile in five seconds. In order for an airplane to break the sound barrier, it has to go faster than that. On October 14, 1947, just under a month after the United States Air Force had been created as a separate service, Charles "Chuck" Yeager in his aircraft christened "Glamorous Glennis" after his wife, broke the sound barrier. He went faster than the speed of sound, broke through the barrier with a loud explosion and left a visual white halo. These halos are formed by condensed water droplets which are thought to drop as a result of a decrease in air pressure around the aircraft.[12]

Breaking through the sound barrier left visible evidence. When we break through any barriers, we become different and will also leave visible proof. Imagine how people felt when they broke the four-minute mile, or how twenty-three-year-old Michael Phelps felt when the eighth gold medal was placed around his neck at the Beijing Olympics in 2008. Imagine how these events changed people's lives and how distinctively different they felt about themselves.

Breaking through our self-sabotage barriers makes us *visually* different. We exude energy and walk with confidence and boldness when we know we are loved and have a significant purpose on this earth. We are able to smile easier when we don't worry over insignificant mistakes, and people love to be around us because of our infectious joy. We will also find that we can boldly pursue new relationships, ministry opportunities or careers.

Risk Grace

If we choose to break the self-sabotage barrier to reach our full potential in how God created us to be, it is absolutely necessary to take risks. Risk always implies possible loss, being frightened of appearing like a fool, or being too vulnerable, sentimental or exposing our true self. But we must take risks because without them we will never break the sabotage barrier of unleashing our true, magnificent self.

For me, the greatest risk in breaking my perfectionism barrier was the understanding that I deserved to receive God's grace. Don't let this simple concept fool you; it is one thing to understand God's grace, but it is another to receive it and let it be the vision through which we see life. It is easier to work at earning love and feeling self-righteous about our progress than to receive God's unconditional love. That kind of love is like going down a zip-line or free falling into a safety net, because our human mind does not understand the word "unconditional." It is hard for us to imagine that God wants all of us traveling on his plane, first class, free. We don't have to be perfect.

Liz Curtis Higgs puts her experience this way, "An enormous bolt of lightning ripped through my delusions and exposed me for the fraud that I was. But it also exposed the power of the cross! Weeping, I threw myself at the grace of a Lord I had claimed but never known."[13]

God never humiliates and condemns us by saying: "See, I told you so." He only says, "I love you so." The sabotage barrier that needs to be broken is our change of heart; a powerful realization that "It is God who arms me with strength and makes my way perfect" (2 Sam. 22:33, NIV).

Grace Breaks the "Nobody" Barrier

What we believe about ourselves determines the quality of choices that we make. If we believe that we are a *nobody*—that we have little value and we don't deserve anything good to happen to us—we will sabotage God's gorgeous grace, abundant generosity and beautiful purpose for our life. But, if we believe that God loves and values us and want us to enjoy who He created us to be, we will know and believe we are a *somebody*.

It is God, not us, who changes a *nobody* into a *somebody*. This is what God said to His people: "In the very place where they were once named Nobody, they will be named God's Somebody" (Hosea 1:10-11, MSG).

And here's how God will do it through us:

1. Pay Attention

One of my very wise bosses told me one day, "Heidi, the best thing you can learn in business is to *pay attention*." That information didn't seem much smarter than a third grader could learn; however, I did pay attention and learned that being aware of something is the first step to making good choices for improvement.

We must become aware of self-sabotage to eliminate it. This is the hardest part because this false belief system is so ingrained in us that we think it is who we are. Let your friends be your mirror to point it out and help you. Better yet, pray and ask God to reveal it to you; because He will. "Here's what I want you to do: Find a quiet, secluded place so you won't be tempted to role-play before God. Just be there as simply and honestly as you can manage. The focus will shift from you to God, and you will begin to sense his grace" (Matt. 6:6, MSG). When we stop manipulating and playing games and get brutally honest with ourselves, it will be the first step in changing sabotage to success.

2. Active Listening

Be aware of the negative self-talk. When we are afraid of some of the sabotaging *therefores* listed above, listen to the words that you have just spoken in your mind. Do they line up with God's unconditional love for you, or do you go back to the default mode that says you don't deserve to live in joy and freedom?

We can't listen properly in the midst of blaring sitcoms on TV, loud music or family chaos. God knows our need to become quiet so that we can hear His voice in our soul. "Are you tired? Worn out? Burned out on religion? Come to me. Get away with me and you'll recover your life. I'll show you how to take a real rest. Walk with me and work with me—watch how I do it" (Matt. 11:28-29, MSG).

When we intentionally listen to God's beautiful words of promises, instead of our defeating self-talk, we will begin to understand what we need to do to recover our life. It will be like sitting quietly under the safety of an umbrella and keeping all the raindrops of lies away from you and resting in the comfort and shelter of God who wants to love and protect you. He uses his arms to watch over you, and shield you—not to harm or destroy you.

3. Do It

As I write this, I have the most adorable, sweet-natured, smart nine-teen-month-old granddaughter. She visited with us for a whole week and I taught her some songs that need actions. One of the songs is:

> "Row, Row, row your boat, gently down the stream,
> Merrily, merrily, merrily, merrily, life is but a dream."

I love to watch her little dimpled hands try to row that boat down the stream. When she is done, she claps her hands, laughs and her blue eyes sparkle with joy and excitement.

I chuckle when I sing this song because I used the words of this nurs-ery rhyme as advice in one of my prayer counseling sessions. I can still see the woman's big puzzled eyes staring back at me, but I think I gave her some great wisdom on self-sabotage. Jesus tells us this: "Learn the unforced rhythms of grace. I won't lay anything heavy or ill-fitting on you. Keep com-pany with me and you'll learn to live freely and lightly" (Matt. 11:30, MSG).

To learn how to live freely and lightly, we have to learn to flow in the "unforced rhythms of grace"—by rowing our boats *down* the stream. We must choose to find those rhythms in life that we were created for, going with the flow of life instead of trying to force things to happen. By rowing *upstream*, we are going against the flow of life and wasting precious energy, time and passion and sabotaging our freedom and the abundant life that God has prepared for us.

You may believe you are the world's *nobody*, but you were created to be God's gorgeous, valuable *somebody*. We may not have done anything in this life to deserve all the goodness that God wants to pour into our lives, but He wants us to have it. Take it. He died for it.

Choices That Enrich Your Life

1. If your false belief system tells you that "life is a disappointing place," choose to override your feelings and go for your goal. Not attaining what we truly believe is designed for us is also disappointing. If you try something and don't attain it, at least you tried.

2. None of us is perfect. Choose to take on a project or new challenge knowing that you will not be able to do it perfectly. Enjoy the journey of the opportunity.

3. Sometimes we pursue careers, goals or activities that are not of our own choosing. Is it because it was something the "Jones" family wanted for you so they could be proud of you? Accomplishing something for other people is sabotaging your own gifts and desires and God's plan for your life. Choose to remain true to yourself.

4. Success may make you fearful that family dynamics will change or your close friends may leave you. We may be afraid other people will become jealous and resentment may build in relationships—and they may. Boldly choose to step into your fear and not sabotage the thrill of writing your first book, singing your first song, going back to school or starting your own business.

5. If you have a belief system that says, "no one can be trusted," reassess what you expect trust to look like in your relationships. Is it realistic? Choose to believe that we are all imperfect people and that on this side of heaven everyone will let us down at one time or another. Choose your relationships carefully and trust anyway.

6. An amazing opportunity has emerged that affirms the use of your gifts and abilities—but you can't afford it. Choose to believe that the God who has placed this passion and opportunity in your life is also the door that opens the way to provide the necessary finances.

7. You have found someone who you believe is right for you, but you are already picking out all the faults that you know will ultimately damage the relationship. Choose to listen to God and ask if these faults are danger signs for an unhealthy relationship, or

are they the beginning of the sabotage of a relationship you feel you don't deserve?

8. You are overweight and struggle with feeling unattractive and unlovable. Choose to believe that you were created to be magnificent. When you begin to make choices on that belief system, you will become beautiful from the inside out and will eventually stop the endless trips to the refrigerator.

9. You are not a victim. Yes, bad things may have happened to you, they happen to all of us; but that does not need to thwart your efforts toward reaching your goals. Choose to take responsibility for all that has happened in your life and move forward to a victimless future.

10. Do you struggle with finding motivation to do what you know you should be doing? This is procrastination and it lets you pretend that you are going to do it someday—just not today. When you keep putting something off, that means you don't have to take responsibility for it… just yet! Choose to do it and you will probably find it was much easier than you thought than it would be, and it will leave you with a sense of accomplishment and fulfillment.

11. You spend so much time taking care of everybody and everything else that there is no time or energy to spend on yourself. Choose to realize that this is a martyrdom attitude and doesn't guarantee you any rewards. Choose to take care of yourself first, so that you can be healthy, joyful and productive and lead a fulfilled, balanced life.

12. Honor the person God made you to be and choose, every day, to be true to your real self.

Stop and Ask God To Help You Change Sand to Pearls

Begin by asking: God, what am I sabotaging?

S Scripture: "No eye has seen, no ear has heard, and no mind has imagined what God has prepared for those who love him. But it was to us that God revealed these things by his Spirit. For his Spirit searches out everything and shows us God's deep secrets" (1 Cor. 2:9-10, NLT).

T Thanksgiving: Thank You, God, that You are fully engaged in my life. I can't even imagine all that You want me to experience in this lifetime. Thank You that You have given me the Holy Spirit that will help me search out and break all the lies that I have been living. Thank You that I don't have to try and do this on my own, but that You will reveal them to me and help me on this journey of discovering who You designed me to be.

O Observation: Everything that God does is good, and I know that God is up to something good in my life. I need to appropriate the power of the Holy Spirit to reveal the truth about myself, and the secrets of God. I realize these are "spirit-filled" discoveries, so it makes sense that my constant joy will come from a fulfilled life from my spirit, not from more "stuff" that is bought, accumulated and eventually discarded.

P Prayer: God, this is huge and complicated and I need Your help. I realize that my thoughts, habits, words and actions have probably come from what I have learned by living in an imperfect world. Help me to discover the lies I have believed and am presently acting on. I do not want to be like the ten spies that held the fruit in one hand and decided to sabotage Your promises of milk and honey. God, give me the courage, wisdom and insight to make the kind of choices that will take me into the beautiful destiny You designed for me. Quicken my heart and whisper to me when I am going down a self-sabotage road once again. Help me to partner with the Holy Spirit within me to navigate wisely through the many choices that I need to make every day. Thank You that You will.

Amen.

Chapter 3

Friendship, Fake or Real Part 1

Heart Songs—Writing the Lyrics

Friends are like rainbows, heartsongs, and life… they are a gift from God.
—MATTIE J. T. STEPANEK, JANUARY, 1997

My girlfriend Fran's voice softened and I could sense she wanted to share something very intimate. She looked intently into my eyes and said, "At that moment it didn't matter if I lived or died; because I had experienced my perfect moment in time." I nodded in agreement. I knew the event she was referring to; it had indeed been captivating. The harmony of laughter and music made us feel as though our hearts would explode with joy. The mixture of friendships were so authentic, beautiful and fun that it could only be imagined as a supernatural collision of heaven and earth: a *heart song*. That day was still vividly clear and fresh for both of us.

That heart song occasion was celebrating my friend Fran's sixtieth birthday. Her husband Bob looked after all the arrangements of treating many of their friends to a day of golfing on a British Columbia golf course that was nothing short of majestic. The course was built on the side of grand towering mountains overlooking the glimmering Mara Lake. Even though each hole on this course was challenging and difficult to master, at every tee box people stopped and gazed in awe at all the splendid beauty.

God was really showing off His creation that day, and it seemed as though we took a peek into heaven.

The sumptuous evening meal was displayed under a crown of stars, mingled with the dancing moonbeams on the glistening lake. Music and laughter were intertwined with heartfelt toasts and birthday wishes to my dear friend Fran. Magic filled the air and it made me say, "I wish we could bottle this and keep it forever!"

Three weeks later a phone call obliterated the enchantment. Fran had been called back to her doctor's office and he had discovered a lump in her breast, ultimately leading to a double mastectomy. The following year was a roller coaster of spending time in doctors' waiting rooms, going through multiple surgeries, needing pain killers and trying to cope with the daily challenges and hindrances.

During the summer of 2009, I sat with Fran and we reflected on what God had brought her through in the last two years. It was tough, but throughout the surgeries, pain and blackness she recalled the night of her sixtieth birthday when all her friends were together to celebrate the sweetness and goodness of her life. We both agreed that God gives us heart song friends and perfect moments in time to give us hope for the darker days ahead. None of us should ever walk through tragedy alone.

Life-Affirming Limbic Dance

We are created for relationship. We throw that cliché around glibly, but it is a fact that intimate relationships are the most fundamental, powerful human need. Being around people we love makes us feel energized, confident, and we know we are accepted and belong. This type of intimate, authentic friendship not only helps us through our dark, emotional trials; it actually helps us to live longer, healthier lives. These friendships cause our brains to do a beautiful, colorful "limbic dance." There is a part of our brain that runs our emotions and it is called the limbic system:

> If you had an MRI, you can actually see it. For every moment you are with someone, your limbic brain is tuning

them in, being changed by their moods, as well as changing theirs too. It is a constant life-affirming limbic dance.
Some people can make you feel better by simply walking
into the room you are in. Directly or unconsciously, these
sorts of interactions (mood sharing) feel very good. Without them, we would wither away.[14]

Daniel Goleman, in his book *Social Intelligence*, explains the correla-
tion between friendships and our health in great detail:

> In one study, a hundred men and women wore devices
> that took readings of their blood pressure whenever they
> interacted with someone. When they were with family or
> enjoyable friends, their blood pressure fell; these interac-
> tions were pleasant and soothing. When they were with
> someone who was troublesome, there was a rise.... Medi-
> cal science has pinpointed a biological mechanism that
> directly links a toxic relationship to heart disease.[15]

I discovered the power of heart song friends when my husband died
two weeks before Christmas and I felt helpless and vulnerable. My friends
became my "heart beats" walking outside of my body. They showed up at
the door to help me with grocery shopping, cleaning my house, answering
the phone and cooking meals. My sister Brigitte slept on a mattress at the
foot of my bed for three weeks, just to make sure I was getting some sleep
and rest. Friends sat with me for hours, with their arms wrapped around me
to hold and comfort me. Sometimes we simply sat in silence with tears running down our faces. Even though I had not lived in Lethbridge, Alberta,
for almost two years, a group of friends from that city rented a bus during
the most stressful and busy time of the year, to drive for hours and show up
at my doorstep the night before the funeral. But the strangest, most captivating and surprising moments came when someone would recall a funny

memory; we would all burst out in refreshing, hilarious laughter. Even in the most painful and grievous experiences, laughing with my friends had the power to break the tension in a room and refresh our hearts. I am sure for that moment in time our brains experienced a heart song and were doing a limbic dance.

God made our bodies to experience the healing and refreshing power of friendships to carry each other through our valleys of death and pain. God knows we need each other, He tells us: "Laugh with your happy friends when they're happy; share tears when they're down. Get along with each other; don't be stuck-up" (Rom. 12:15, MSG). There is no medical prescription, therapy or counseling that will provide better healing than having friends who will share our laughter and validate our tears and fears.

Heart Songs—Writing Beautiful Lyrics

Today we need friendships more than ever. A hundred years ago before we had TV, radio and internet, people sat and talked to each other for stimulation and entertainment. Today, a lot of our stimulus comes from technology and trying to keep up with too many activities and too much information. But, relationships are becoming increasingly important as more people are single either by choice or circumstance and do not have a family structure. Very few families live together and share their life experiences and stories. They are spread out all over the world and connect through e-mail, Skype, Twitter, Facebook or the occasional phone call and visit. These are all good communication tools, but they cannot replace the powerful human touch and retrieve the life-affirming energy drawn from looking into each other's eyes. Many families are juggling too many home responsibilities, activities and careers that expect them to work long hours, do shift work or travel. Opportunities to spend time together are being crushed by the onslaught of the never-ending demands in this twenty-first century.

We have a generation that is slipping into living in isolation. We live in gated communities; we have garage door openers, and "drive-through" everything. We no longer take the time to linger on our front porches or walk and chat with neighbors in the evenings.

These are legitimate obstacles that make heart song connections more difficult but more critical than ever. We need more than just surface friendships or acquaintances; we need friendships that say, "I know just what you mean. I hear your words; but I also hear your heart." It is life-affirming for us when we can finish each other's sentences and exclaim, "You too? Me too!"

One of the most popular sitcoms of the Nineties was *Friends*. It ran from 1994 to 2004, and the finale was watched by 52.5 million people.[16] I believe we are all curious what it feels like to have a group of friends that accept us just the way we are. We long to have someone celebrate and share our victories. More importantly, we need to know there is someone who will be there with us when a knock on the door or a phone call turns our world upside down.

Our greatest joy emerges when we are in loving, accepting and flourishing friendships. These are not simply my words, they are also Jesus' words to us just before He went to the cross and talked to the disciples about how He wanted us to live: "I've told you these things for a purpose: that my joy might be your joy, and your joy wholly mature. This is my command: Love one another the way I loved you. This is the very best way to love. Put your life on the line for your friends" (John 15:15, MSG).

It is a spiritual and physical fact that we will indeed experience no greater joy in our life than when we learn to live in a relationship with an intimate, trustworthy and healthy love.

When I do a workshop or conference on the power of friendship, one question that I always ask the attendants is, "Who will you call at 2:00 in the morning?" When I had to call a friend in the middle of the night, I realized how vital it is to have someone that you can count on when life takes an ugly turn. You find out who your real friends are when you feel pathetic and need a shoulder to cry on. I am always surprised and saddened to find how many women do not have a heart song friend. So many women come to me with tears in their eyes and ask, "How can I have a 2:00 in the morning friendship?" We crave this kind of friendship, but we are all such complex, unique people, that there is not one easy answer for this simple and short question. The saying "if you want to have a friend, you have to be a friend" seems logical, but how do we actually do this? There are several key lyrics that develop and maintain loving heart song friendships.

1. Lyrics of Time

I have found that in our North American culture the biggest obstacle and threat to having heart song friendships is time. Two sentences that I hear more than anything are:

     i. "I don't have time."
     ii. "I'm too busy."

I have a friend who asks, "How do you spell love?" Then with a smile on her face she gives us the answer: "T.I.M.E." Unfortunately time is the only way to cultivate, nurture and maintain any relationship; whether it is a heart song friendship, family relations, marriage or our relationship with God. Also, too often we use these excuses to justify failing to get together or being afraid to make ourselves vulnerable and commit to building an authentic relationship. I think a lot of us take our friends for granted and hope they will be there for us the next time we need them. Taking the time to invest in friendships with people and with God is even more valuable than investing our time in building our bank account and our material possessions. Our bank account will not comfort us or talk to us when we are lonely or need someone to put their arms around our shoulders.

When I spoke in Yellowknife, in the Northwest Territories in 2008, I was delighted to meet many of the women that came down by boat and bus from the most northern part of the province from the area of Fort McPherson. It was easy to fall in love with these Gwich'in women with their big smiles, beautiful wrinkled faces and loving, accepting hearts. These women know about heartache. Many mothers shared stories of losing their sons to drowning in the Peel River or the McKenzie Delta during the spring thaw when the ice was breaking up. My first question to them was, "Do you have a friend that can walk alongside you during your time of pain and grief?" They always responded with a puzzled look on their faces and answered, "Of course I have friends; many friends." It was a revelation to me to discover that they don't seem to struggle with the North American obstacle of friendships: time. In the North Country they have a lot of time during the winter when it is dark for twenty-four hours. They have the time, or make the time, to develop friendships and walk with each other through their life's hardships.

Stephen Lungu, a director of African Enterprise said, "In Africa people have lots of time and no stuff. Here in America we have lots of stuff but no time." It made me so sad to hear that because it made me realize we do seem to value stuff and accomplishments over spending time with people we love. Time is the foundation for the next steps that I will list, but without investing in this first step, we can throw the rest of the suggestions out of the window.

2. Lyrics of Listening, Not Fixing

In all the research I have done on friendships, the evidence is clear: everyone craves for someone to simply listen to them. This sounds basic, but it's hard to do if we don't take the time. In her book *Friendshifts*, the author Dr. Jan Yager agrees that this is an important ingredient:

> One of the best ways to be a better best, close or casual friend is through improved *listening skills*. Your friends may want to hear about your triumphs, wows and every day goings-on, but they are usually even *more* interested in telling you about what is happening in their lives. The more you sincerely listen to your friends, the more your friends are pulled toward you. Being sympathetic toward your friend's point of view or situation, and showing empathy, is one way to achieve better listening skills.[17]

When someone really listens to us, not just with their ears but with their heart, it makes us believe we are valuable enough to be heard. I remember a conversation I had with my heart song friend Shaunie about six years ago. I was going through an extremely stressful time where the demands on my time exceeded my ability to meet expectations and deadlines. I couldn't blame anyone except myself for the overburdened, overscheduled mess I found myself in. As I poured out all my frustrations and eventually ended up in tears, she listened. She didn't chastise me for getting myself into this predicament; she didn't try to help me fix it, or give me a pat answer or a quick fix prayer. She just listened. When I got off the phone I felt so much lighter, and peaceful. Looking back, I realize it was because she validated my struggle simply by listening.

What an incredible gift we can give each other: to open the windows of our soul to each other when we listen. When we do this, we are bearing each other's burdens. "Be completely humble and gentle; be patient, *bearing* with one another in love" (Eph. 4:2, NIV, italics mine). One of the Greek verbs for "bear" is *enecho*, "to hold up."[18] What a beautiful description; one friend holding another one up and loving each other simply by extending an ear.

The author of *A Woman and Her Relationships*, Rosemary Flaaten, talks about bearing by saying, "Bearing with one another is not attempting to fix each other. Bearing is being attentive and present in the relationship, truly listening to what the other is sharing rather than formatting and rehearsing how we'll respond, setting aside our interests and preoccupations, accepting the other's place and encouraging her to become all that God desires her to be."[19]

The first two lyrics will be the door that opens heart song friendships. The next few steps will help them to flourish and keep them maintained.

3. Write Creative Lyrics

For any relationship to flourish, we have to keep it fresh, creative, fun and moving forward. This is an essential step that takes time, effort and creativity. Without this step any relationship will become stagnant and die a slow death.

In his book, *Vital Friends*, the author Tom Rath reveals that we also need to focus on what each person is contributing to our friendships. That means that we should not expect one or two friends to meet all our needs and expectations. He tells us that there needs to be different friends for the critical roles and needs in our life. "The problem is, friendships are not designed to be well-rounded; 83% of the people we have studied report that they bring different strengths to the relationship than their best friend does."[20]

My friend Lesley-Ann shares her story about her quest to find that one friend that would fulfill every area of her life:

> When I was a little girl I had dreams. Like other little girls, I dreamed that I would someday become a teacher, or an artist, or a veterinarian, or even a heroine in a fantastic story. I also dreamed of having a best friend—someone who understood me completely. Like Anne Shirley in *Anne of Green Gables*, I longed for a "bosom friend" with whom I could share life, through thick and through thin.
>
> This notion of having a bosom friend affected many relationship decisions I made growing up. I trusted and then mistrusted females in my life that didn't fulfill my vision. My childish fantasy of finding one ultimately fulfilling relationship haunted me, causing pain and broken relationships.
>
> At the midpoint in my life, I finally know that God never planned for me to place a best bosom friend on a pedestal. No girlfriend, husband or child is meant to be there. That place is reserved for God alone, who wants to be my best friend forever. So, I'm trying to lean into that truth, and remove the pressure of my needs from my human friends. With God in his rightful place, I now see that He has given me not one, but a beautiful plethora of female friends that fill my life with humor, grace, wisdom, soul-wrenching honesty and spiritual

connectivity. They arrive in my life at precisely the right time,
placed there for whatever God needs me to learn, change,
grow in or go through.[21]

We all need different groups of friends through which we can experience the various interests and activities that we are involved in. I love and value each one of my friends for the wonderful, unique gifts they bring into my life.

> i. Accountability Group—My "Sacred Socks Friends"
> For the last several years I have developed a deep accountability friendship with two beautiful women. It started as a Bible study where we chose to study A.W. Tozer's book called *The Pursuit of God*. This challenging book called us to become authentic before God and each other; and that became the foundation of what we chose to accomplish. One evening as we arrived I brought some soft fuzzy socks with me so that our feet wouldn't get cold on the hardwood floor. Since that time we put on our fuzzy socks as we study, eat, laugh, share stories and then end the evening in a beautiful, powerful prayer time. These times with my Sacred Socks friends have dramatically changed my life, as we have become *spiritually naked and not ashamed* to share our dreams, fears, guilt and struggles. When we expose the innermost parts of our soul with someone, and then together lay them at the cross of Jesus through prayer, there is a soul connection that unites hearts through the beauty and power of the Holy Spirit like nothing else on this earth.
>
> Authenticity with God and with each other has been the powerful link that has melted our hearts and given us a bond to help us grow together. We have given each other permission to ask some hard questions:
> - "Were you jealous in there?"
> - "What makes you feel prideful?"

- "Your life seems really busy. Are you sure all your priorities are in order?"
- "Is this your idea, or do you believe it is a part of God's plan for your life?"
- "How much time are you spending in solitude with God?"

We all need someone who will look us in the eye and ask us some thought-provoking questions. It is the only way that we can be held accountable to learn and grow to be magnificent people.

My question to you is: "Would you be courageous enough to *choose* one or two women that you would be willing to become authentic with and hold each other accountable?" A relationship where God is in the middle will fill your soul and empower your relationships in a way you would never imagine possible.

ii. Fun and Creative Group—The "Birthday Group"

We all need a circle of friends that bring out the fun and creative side of our life. It is vitally important to have people in our life we can be silly with, laugh with and accept each other with all our unique and different personalities. I have such a group that I cherish and love and look forward to each "birthday celebration." We have been doing this for about twelve years, and even though some people have come and gone, moved away or moved away from us, we continue to intentionally pursue and plan our times together. We have shared our sorrows, cheered when someone achieved their university degree and celebrated the birth of my first book, *Beauty Unleashed: Transforming a Woman's Soul*. We went through the process of one of our friends adopting a child from Ethiopia. We have been thrilled to celebrate this magnificent journey and are learning how to include that child as part of our friendship family. We have tried different restaurants, helped to remodel some rooms in our houses, eaten in each other's homes and encouraged each other through hardships. Even though we are all different and a little quirky, it is a picture of a beautiful tapestry, a little rumpled and fuzzy on the backside, but beautifully formed through shared laughter, love and acceptance.

We all need a friendship group where we can share common interests. Whether it is a book club, a hiking group, golfing friends, scrapbooking, cooking or walking friends; we all need a circle of friends who we can laugh with and with whom we can celebrate life's defining moments.

My question to you is: "Will you look around and *choose to* belong to a creative circle of friends who will celebrate you and laugh with you?"

iii. Learning Group—"My Study Groups"

People who continue to learn are refreshing, interesting and keep us challenged to keep growing as well. For over twenty-five years I have been involved in some type of a study group, growing in leadership, speaking, teaching and, most importantly for me, learning about God's word in the Bible. The place where we grow the most is amongst a group of people where we share our lives and study and learn. This group may start out where people are merely acquaintances, but over time some of these people can become your heart song friends as you share your life's stories of struggles and hope. There are so many wonderful opportunities to find a place to connect with other people to expand your thinking.

My question to you is: "Will you be bold and *choose* to sign up for a study course so that you can learn and grow with like-minded people? They may start out as strangers, but someone may end up as a lifelong friend.

iv. Laughter

As I am writing this chapter, it is the middle of the Christmas season of 2009. This year, instead of cards, I am writing letters to my children and my heart song friends. As I ponder about what I am going to write, some key elements and events keep emerging. These were occasions where we made intentional time to be together to create memories. The components were: Making time, creating an event (sometimes a little outrageous), being authentic and laughing. I still laugh when I recall sliding on green garbage bags down the snow banks at the back of our yard. The hilarious laughter that emerged from that zany event keeps us talking about it for years.

We desperately need laughter in our relationships; I believe it breaks down barriers, tension and offenses. Laughter brings pleasure that makes our brain do the colorful, limbic dance. After a good bout of laughter, the kind that makes us double over and have tears streaming down our faces, it actually has the potential to heal us. If you remember the movie *Patch Adams*, it was the ground-breaking blockbuster movie that showed the concept of humor and laughter as a healing power. We need friends to help us laugh. We must never forget that friends are God's gift to us, but it is up to you and me to unwrap the individual gift boxes. You never know, inside one of these boxes you could find a heart song friend.

Lesley-Ann continues to tell us how friends are God's gift to us:

This morning I had coffee with a vibrant, beautiful young girlfriend. We sat and talked about relationships and jobs and the economy. And, though we didn't reach any profound conclusions, a shift took place—new hope and energy began to percolate inside me as I headed out the door for home.

God has splashed the canvas of my life with a colorful collection of women who overwhelm me with their friendship and love. My understanding of what it means to be a friend is wider because of their witty and serious, gracious and goofy, energetic and organized, wise and spiritual, artistic and analytical, youthful and seasoned selves. My life is rich and fun because they are all my friends. I thank God for these gifts because I would be lost without them.[22]

Choices That Enrich Your Life

1. You believe you don't know how to be a friend; this was never modeled for you as you were growing up. Choose to step out and take some risks. Anything that we set out to do that we have never done before entails risk and possible rejection. Ask God to help you step by step as you tenderly open the door to this new and exciting territory. Dale Carnegie has four simple guidelines to winning a friend:
   a. Smile.
   b. Arouse in the other person an eager want.
   c. Give honest, sincere appreciation.
   d. Avoid criticizing.[23]

2. How do you know who will make a good friend? Choose to look around and find someone that you know will be able to share your interests. The greatest predictor in longevity of friendships is having shared values.

3. You are afraid that if you disclose information to other people, one day they may use it against you and hurt you. Choose to know this is a possibility. That is why it is so crucial to know who your heart song friend is versus your casual friend. You have to build up a trust factor before you share your soul.

4. Everyone seems so busy these days, how in the world do we make time for friendships? Choose to believe that God has given each of us twenty-four hours in a day and you are the only one who has the power to choose how you will spend it. Find someone that you know will find your friendship valuable enough to make the time.

If it is a friend that will not go out of their way to make time, they are not your friend.

5. Can Facebook and Twitter help you to build relationships? Choose to believe we are people who need to be touched and have conversations where we are eyeball to eyeball so that we can look into the windows of our hearts. Facebook and Twitter are wonderful tools for keeping in touch with people about our daily activities, but they will not be able to help us with the intimate, grueling details of our life.

6. You and your friend seem to be drifting apart. Should you just let go? Choose to believe that God brings friends into our life for a reason and for a season. If you are drifting apart it could be for a number of reasons:

   a. Neither of you have maintained your friendship by helping each other to flourish. Now your relationship has become stagnant.

   b. There is unresolved hurt and it seems easier to pull away than to deal with it.

   c. You are simply growing apart by having different interests, jobs, churches or recreational activities.

   d. You have found other friends.

7. Is it good to have a heart song friendship in a workplace? Tom Rath in his book *Vital Friends* tells us that we are seven times more productive when we have a good friend in our workplace. But we have to be aware that this can cause complications when conflict arises in the workplace or the friendship. Choose to treat this friendship wisely and be aware that it can cause jealousy among other employees, and if the friendship begins to falter, you are stuck with each other on a daily basis.

8. Can you be good friends with a member of the opposite sex? This one always causes controversy and great discussions. From what I have observed, this can be healthy for a time, but at one point or another, one of you will begin to feel things that go beyond the

friendship boundaries. Beautiful, healthy relationships that start as friendship can lead to a great marriage. Choose to be alert and recognize that an intimate friendship with the opposite sex can get complicated.

9. Can your heart song friend be your husband? Of course he can, and how wonderful that would be, but please remember that men and women think differently. Women need to talk about everything that is going on in their lives and some men simply don't understand how women think. Choose to believe that yes, your husband should be your best friend, but he will not always be interested in the fact that you got a pair of earrings on sale, or how excited you are about the different color of your new toenail polish. That is why we have girlfriends.

10. You don't have any groups where you belong, that will help you to be creative and celebrate your life. Please choose to go and find some. Women can be relentless in finding a pair of shoes to match a new outfit, or a book we want to read, or new pillows for the couch. Please use that same tenacity in locating a common interest group. There are endless organizations in every city for recreational or learning activities where you can meet great people who share the same values and interests as you.

Stop and Ask God To Help You Change Sand to Pearls

Begin by asking: God, how can I be a heart song friend?

S Scripture: "Be completely humble and gentle; be patient, bearing with one another in love" (Eph. 4:2, NIV).

T Thanksgiving: Thank You, God, that You give us the gift of friendship. Thank You that this beautiful love has the ability to hold us up during painful struggles in our life. It is amazing to me that these friendships can actually help us to flourish and live longer. God, I stand in awe as to how You created our bodies so magnificently. Thank You.

O Observation: When we bear each other's burdens and hold each other up in love, we have the power to live healthy, joyful lives. I need to learn to be that kind of friend to others.

P Prayer: God, You have indeed made us so that our greatest joy comes when we are in loving relationships. I confess that I do not always know how to do this. I need Your help so that I can make intentional time to spend with my friends. God, teach me how to listen. I want to be the kind of friend that not only hears with my ears, but also with my heart, so that I validate my friends' words simply by listening. Help me also to realize that relationships are the most important thing I can invest in while I am living on this earth. I need to remind myself that ultimately everything will one day fade away, but the breath of God will one day join us in eternity. Teach me how to be in an intimate, loving relationship with You, God, and then with my heart song friends.

Amen.

Chapter 4

Friendship, Fake or Real Part 2

Heart Songs—Nurturing Hearts

> *Friendship is born at the moment when one person says to another,*
> *"What! You too? I thought I was the only one."*
>
> —C.S. LEWIS

I am sure that we have all had near death experiences. I can vividly recall several of my own. Most of them happened on a dark, gloomy night when I was tired and anxious to get home after an exhausting day at work. One particular black night the rain pelted so hard, and the windshield wipers were moving so fast, that I could barely see the cars in front of me. I signaled to turn into the left lane and in that instant I made eye contact with a horrified, drenched biker who missed my car by a breath. I gasped! My heart pounded and I was frantic as the sharp reality hit me that I almost killed him. I was sure I had looked carefully to my left before changing lanes, but I almost ran over him. How could I not see him? There was another startling incident when I found headlights coming directly toward me and I almost had a head-on collision. Both times I was sure I checked all my directions and mirrors; how could my eyes have missed these life-threatening dangers?

Nurturing Hearts

1. Scotoma Busters

We all suffer from scotomas. These are areas of diminished vision more commonly known as blind spots. We need trusted friends in our lives who will be our "scotoma busters"; in fact our lives depend on them. To reach our full potential, we cannot do without friends who love us enough to show us things we can't see ourselves. We need someone we can trust enough to be the eyes in the back of our heads; to protect our backs from the things that have the potential to harm us or even kill us. We need their loyalty and boldness to be able to tell us when:

- They see warning signs in our relationships that foretell impending disaster.
- We drink too much, take the wrong drugs, read too much junk, or overindulge in food. Good friends know when we are on the dreadful road of gaining weight and they need to be able to stop us before it gets to the point of no return.
- We have said hurtful, irreparable words to other people.
- We respond with jealousy.
- We spend too much.
- We are about to make a bad choice.

It takes time, vulnerability, trust and loyalty to nurture this type of friendship. Hardly anyone has more power and ability to shape us into Christ-like character than these beautiful people.

2. Lid and Grid Removers

We also need someone to expand our horizons, teach us to identify the gifts God has given us, embrace opportunities and enlarge our perspective on life. These are our lid and grid removers.

Many of us have heard of the fleas that were put in a jar and kept trying to jump out but continuously bumped into the lids. Even after the lid was taken off, the fleas only jumped as high as the lids. They had learned that "this is as high as I can go." The same principle applies to grids. We have learned to function by seeing life through our own patterned grids and we feel comfortable operating in this predictable and fairly safe environment. How amazing and refreshing when we develop friendships with people who will gently remove our lids, enlarge our grids and help us to courageously pursue our dreams and cheer us on to explore new and exciting territories. These friends have the capability to change our perspective on life, shove us out of our banal comfort zones and help us map out the dreams God puts in our hearts to make a difference in our areas of influence, or even the world. We need someone to say:

- "You can do it, because God has given you the passion, the gift, and now I am here to help you go for it."
- "What is the worst thing that can happen to you?"
- "Come on now, just because there is a little bump in the road, don't give up."
- "I believe in you, and I'll be here with you all the way."

It is difficult to sojourn through life without someone to help us discover new terrain. Some of their ideas may sound radical because they have never been part of your "grid thinking," but don't dismiss them without giving them prayerful consideration. God gives us these extra sets of eyes to help us to risk seeing His magnificent world through a bigger perspective.

3. Give Mulligans

Many relationships are abandoned because of misunderstandings and mistakes. This usually happens because of unmet expectations and differences of opinion, which are an inevitable part of all relationships. We want our best friends to be able to read our thoughts, and in our minds we selfishly play the game of "I'll meet your needs if you meet mine." When these unspoken expectations are not met we feel that our friends have let us down and we can no longer trust them.

Golfing with my husband and friends is probably one of my favorite recreational activities in the summertime. Some of my most memorable

snapshots in life have been taken while golfing with friends in South Caro-
lina, Hawaii, or some of the beautiful golf courses in British Columbia,
Canada. Some of these courses are tough, and because I am not familiar
with their layout, I don't know what lies around the next corner and where
to place my next shot. Often I get into a rough spot where it's difficult to
hit from, or I'll make a horrible shot that gets me into an even bigger mess.
I love it when I golf with friends who are gracious and generous enough to
say, "Hey Heidi, just take a mulligan." That tells me that I don't have to
count that swing and they are overlooking that mistake. That is *unexpected
grace* and we need to extend it freely in all friendships.

The Bible tells it this way: "Accept one another, then, just as Christ
accepted you, in order to bring praise to God" (Rom. 15:7, NIV). The noun
for "accept" in Greek is *charis,* "grace, indicating favor on the part of the
giver, thanks on the part of the receiver."[24] I absolutely love this explanation
of a mulligan: *giving grace to each other simply as a favor, without deserving it.*
That is what we need to with the day-to-day misunderstandings and unmet
expectations before they build up into resentment: give each other mulligans.

It is the most amazing experience when we finally realize we have discovered a heart song friend; but that is only the beginning of the story. The
degree of health in our relationships is directly connected to the degree of
our daily joy. I believe friendships should not only be maintained; we need
to help each other flourish.

4. Pray for Each Other

If you have the kind of friendship where you feel comfortable and free
enough to pray with each other, then you are indeed blessed. My friend
Cheryl tells about the power of prayer in friendship:

> Women need close friends who will carry us through dif-
> ficult seasons of our lives, especially during the season
> of motherhood. Motherhood is an incredibly rewarding
> time in a woman's life; however it can also be one of the

loneliest. I like being a mom, but there are days when I would like to put my children up for sale or take the time to indulge in my own temper tantrum.

I have met many mothers who are hungry for real friendship, but it is difficult to find. I don't mean the kind of friendship where we only e-mail or text or have coffee once a week, but the kind where your friend knows your thoughts and really listens when you are speaking. We long for the kind of friend who makes us feel like she is our long lost sister.

I am blessed because I have my girlfriend Kathryn. Kathryn and I have many things in common: our spouses both work in careers that serve their community/country, we both have boys, both love to cook, and we both have sisters that can sometimes make us crazy. We both love the Lord and desire our children to know and serve the Lord one day. The commonalities of our life certainly help us to be good friends, however, it is the time we have spent praying together that has truly bonded us as sisters in Christ. Kathryn and I have something many people don't and that is an open door and open phone line policy. The most important part of our relationship is that we intentionally make time for each other and pray together.[25]

When, together, we bring our dreams, struggles and misunderstandings to the cross and say each other's names during prayer, it has the power to change our perspective. This is the place where unreal and unmet expectations lose their power, and the gift of *unexpected grace* becomes real.

Heart Groups

I often have women ask me, "What is the difference between a good friend and an acquaintance? Should I work on my many acquaintances to make them my good friends? How do I know what is what?" I don't have the specific answer for that, but Jesus is always my best model of every type of relationship. He connected with people from all groups of life and was able to cross all social, economical and religious barriers. He knew just how He belonged in each space:

1. Multitudes

    a. Jesus: He knew how to function amongst crowds of people. He moved among them, spoke to them, had compassion on them; but he moved on. He didn't try to build a personal and intimate relationship with all of them.

    b. You and Me: We also encounter multitudes. We go to hockey games, football games, golf courses, concerts, community events and other places where there are a lot of people. Here we might enjoy their company, the laughter, and the commonality of the event, but that is where it ends. These are our acquaintances and will probably never be our best friends.

2. The Seventy-Two

    a. Jesus: "After this the Lord appointed seventy-two others and sent them two by two ahead of him to every town and place where he was about to go" (Luke 10:1, NIV). Jesus chose seventy-two people to go out and help Him spread God's love.

    b. You and Me: We also have groups of about seventy-two in our social lives. This is the church for many of us: a place of community where we grow to love God and each other and learn how to use the gifts God has given us. For you this might be a golf course, your workplace, your neighborhood, yacht club or some other social club. This is a place where you can discover your gifts and how you can use them to make a difference in others' lives. Here you may become "friendly" with people, start to ask about their family and children, but you probably don't see them outside of this social environment.

3. The Twelve

a. Jesus: "One of those days Jesus went out to a mountainside to pray, and spent the night praying to God. When morning came, he called his disciples to him and chose twelve of them" (Luke 6:12-13, NIV). This is where it starts to become intimate and where we begin to share and become vulnerable with each other. For the next three years Jesus was with these people almost twenty-four hours a day; they became His family. He "did life" with them.

b. You and Me: Did you notice that Jesus prayed all night before He chose His twelve disciples? This is a significant group of people for us and I believe it is vitally important that we also pray about who these vital people will be. They will probably be the people you share a Bible Study with, go with to movies and dinner, spend summer evenings on the deck with, share with in family gatherings and begin to explore and exchange more private information. I see this group as being on a long social date. They begin to share experiences and nurture an interest in other people's lives, but are still careful about sharing too many of their feelings and thoughts. They have not yet developed the loyalty and trust that is needed in heart song relationships. If this is your group in your local church, these people have a powerful potential to help you become a disciple of Jesus Christ, by spurring you on in your spiritual journey. "And let us consider how we may spur one another on toward love and good deeds. Let us not give up meeting together, as some are in the habit of doing, but let us encourage one another" (Heb. 10:24-25, NIV). As you grow and learn to trust each other, one or two of these have the potential to become a friend in the next group.

4. The Three

a. Jesus: It doesn't say how Jesus picked his inner circle of three men, but He gives us glimpses of intimate moments. Peter,

James and John went with Jesus to a mountain where they shared the most profound moment of their lives. They saw Jesus being transfigured; His face shone like the sun and His clothes became as white as light. Then they heard the voice of His Heavenly Father saying, "This is my Son, whom I love; with him I am well pleased. Listen to him!" (Matt. 17:5, NIV). They also witnessed Jesus walking on water, and raising Lazarus from the dead. These are profound, life-changing moments that only a few people are privy to. Once we share these Holy Spirit experiences, a soul connection takes place in our hearts and ultimately changes the dynamics of a relationship.

b. You and Me: These are our heart song friends that we would trust with our lives. These friends are faithful, tender, reliable, and with whom we share the same values. These are the people to whom we open the window of our souls, and have learned to feel safe enough to share every area of our life and still feel loved and accepted. These relationships are authentic, and we feel safe to share all our shame, guilt and disappointments. We have built enough trust so that we are not afraid to share naked information.[26] We are incredibly blessed if we have two or three of these friends in our lifetime. These are the type of friends we call at 2:00 in the morning because we know they would drop everything to show up and be by our side. God gives us these people to be His arms of love and words of encouragement during our struggles and to help us laugh hilariously during our victories and accomplishments. I believe God gives us these friends so that we can catch glimpses of *perfect moments in time*, and experience His unconditional love and a foretaste of heaven. These people are a gift to us so that we can become more Christ-like, but also so that they can help us when we are overwhelmed with sorrow.

5. One on One

    a. Jesus: Let's follow Jesus to see how He dealt with his friends when He experienced the greatest heartbreak of His life:

        i. He took his group of twelve and went to a quiet place. "Then Jesus went with his disciples to a place called Gethsemane, and he said to them, 'Sit here while I go over there and pray'" (Matt. 26:36, NIV).

        ii. He wanted all twelve with him, but then as He became increasingly sorrowful, He only wanted his closest three. "He took Peter and the two sons of Zebedee along with him, and he began to be sorrowful and troubled" (Matt. 26:37, NIV).

        iii. Then when He became *overwhelmed* with sorrow, He still needed his closest friends. What He needed them to do at this crucial time was to stay close by with him and pray while He talked to His Heavenly Father in solitude and privacy. "'My soul is overwhelmed with sorrow to the point of death. Stay here and keep watch with me'" (Matt. 26:38, NIV).

    b. You and Me: This is my greatest example for determining my groups of friends and how to deal with life's tough experiences. We are so fortunate if we have our *twelve* who will walk with us and share life's experiences. When trouble knocks on our door, it is vitally important for us to have those *three* who will show up and determine to help us with our greatest need. These are the friends that will fling themselves on us and tell us, "I love you enough to stop you from making this foolish choice." They are our heart song friends who we know will pray for us and sojourn with us through our tough seasons. But, sadly, there comes a time when we cannot even depend on our closest *three* to meet our needs. When we are *overwhelmed with sorrow to the point of death,* no one can help us but our Heavenly Father. This is a critical time when we are in so much pain that even our most trusted

and loyal friends will not be able to give us what we need.
As a matter of fact, we have to be careful and know that this
is where our friends may actually hurt us by saying or doing
the wrong thing. We all grieve differently, and none of us
know how to meet each other's needs when we experience
overwhelming pain. At this point no one can help us but our
Heavenly Father. He will be the only one who can feel our
anguish—the kind where we feel like we have been torn apart
by a wild beast. He is the one who created us and knows
us inside and out, and He is the only one who can heal our
broken hearts. We need to be in our own "garden place of
solitude" with our Heavenly Father, but we also need to know
that our friends are close by, praying for us.

Triple-Braided Hearts

There are people on this earth that will rub us like sandpaper and we
will do everything to avoid them. We really would like to give them a
mulligan when they annoy us, but the fact remains that we would rather
look the other way when we run into them because we don't want them
in our lives.

Kerry and Chris Shook explain it this way: "As uncomfortable or unset-
tling as we may find it, God intentionally places some people in our lives to
rub us the wrong way, to smooth the rough edges of our character, so that
we're more like Jesus. Its part of His plan to make my character strong and
steady, so God allows people and pressure to build my character."[27]

We don't like being around these people because they have the power to
bring out all our ugly thoughts and feelings. But we get a whole new perspective when we realize that these people have the potential to teach us something. Instead of looking the other way and taking them off our Christmas
card list and social events, we need to ask ourselves some questions:

    a. "What insecurity button is this pushing in me to make me
       react this way?"

    b. "What true, ugly colors are they revealing about me?"

    c. "God, what are you trying to teach me through this annoyance?"

We have to realize that we all have the capability to annoy each other, but oftentimes it goes deeper than that. With the joys of having heart song friends come the dangers of being betrayed, rejected, overlooked or sometimes even discarded like a useless piece of clothing. We will all be hurt at one time or another in life; that is a fact. We can agree with David when he cried in anguish, "If an enemy were insulting me, I could endure it; if a foe were raising himself against me, I could hide from him. But it is you, a man like myself, my companion, my close friend, with whom I once enjoyed sweet fellowship as we walked with the throng at the house of God" (Psalm 55:12-14, NIV).

How do we endure and overcome this kind of anguish and disloyalty with people we thought were our heart song friends? May I suggest that every relationship needs to be made up of three people so that it will endure these misunderstandings, jealousies, broken trust and betrayal. I believe there are so many broken relationships, divorces, wars and disjointed families because we have not humanly grasped the supernatural power of forgiveness and reconciliation. Jesus died to reconcile the world to God, and man to man. I think that many times it is even easier to accept our forgiveness and reconciliation with God than it is to forgive someone that has deeply rejected and hurt us. We need a third person to help us.

"Two are better than one, because they have a good return for their work: If one falls down, his friend can help him up. But pity the man who falls and has no one to help him up! Also, if two lie down together, they will keep warm. But how can one keep warm alone? Though one may be overpowered, two can defend themselves. A cord of three strands is not quickly broken" (Ecc. 4:9-12, NIV).

A heart song friendship that will endure all storms is made up of: You, a trusted friend and God. We need God in there as the third person so that we can exercise the most critical component in a friendship; forgiveness. (See Epilogue on forgiveness). Forgiveness is not just a nice option, it is a command that Jesus gives us: "If you forgive those who sin against you, your heavenly Father will forgive you. But if you refuse to forgive others, your Father will not forgive your sins" (Matt, 6:14-15, NLT). Don't callously overlook the "but" in that verse; it is the bridge for healing forgiveness and harmony in your life, or the trap door to broken relationships and bitterness. We need three people in order to experience life to the fullest. In spite of the possibility of unfaithfulness and ultimate pain, we need our friends; we were not created to live in isolation.

Chris McCandless, a young man from Atlanta, Georgia, decided he no longer wanted to be poisoned by civilization and all its duplicity. "After graduating from Emory University, top student and athlete Christopher McCandless abandons his possessions, gives his entire $24,000 savings account to charity and hitchhikes to Alaska to live in the wilderness."[28] He fled there to become lost in the wild to shed all false hindrances and find true happiness. In the cold of the winter he died alone and here are two entries in his journals:

- "Some people feel like they don't deserve love. They walk away quietly into empty spaces, trying to close the gaps of the past."
- "Happiness is real when shared."[29]

Everything in life will pass away. The only thing we can nurture on this earth is relationships. In each of us is the "breath of God," which is the only thing we can take with us when we leave this earth. Heart song friendships are the ultimate gift. Go after them.

Choices That Enrich Your Life

1. "You don't understand how deeply my friend (husband, child, neighbor, employer, family) has hurt me." I hear this quotation so often and the only answer I have is, *choose to forgive*. Life is unfair, but there is no other option than forgiveness.

2. "I am afraid that if I disclose information to other people they may one day use it against me and hurt me." Choose to know this is a

possibility. That is why it is so crucial to know who your *heart song* friend is vs. your casual friend. You have to build up a trust factor before you share your soul.

3. "I went through an extremely painful time and my best friend never showed up." Choose to believe that some people don't know how to deal with other people's struggles. Some disappear because they don't know how to help or are too selfish to expend the time and energy to walk alongside someone in trouble. When we are going through a crisis, we really find out who our friends are. When my husband died, it felt as though my friends were being put through a sieve. Some rose to the top, and some simply faded away. Unfortunately the death of a loved one is a defining time to find out who your friends are.

4. "I really am busy. I am at that time in my life where I am juggling a career, driving my children to endless activities, and I rarely even have time for myself. How do I invest in friendships?" Look around for like-minded people in your workplace, your church or your recreational activities. Choose to make the most of your time by integrating a friendship into an activity you are already involved in.

5. "I have betrayed a friend and have asked for her forgiveness, but she refuses to give it to me. What now?" Reconciliation happens only when both parties agree to forgive. I had this exact incident happen to me a number of years ago when I asked a friend for forgiveness and her words were, "Heidi, I will never forgive you." I had to learn to live with that response. Choose to make sure that you have asked for forgiveness and that your heart and motives are pure before God. Then choose to surrender that unresolved pain to God.

6. "I seem to have a lot of acquaintances but no heart song friends." I know of no other way to develop these friendships than the investment of time. Choose to make time.

7. "I would really like to start praying with my friends, but it seems awkward." Praying is like building muscles in a gym. You just have to do it in order to get better at it. Choose to develop your own

prayer life in such a way that it becomes comfortable for you. There may come a point in a conversation with a friend where you can stop and say, "That is a tough question; I don't know the answer. Let's stop and pray and ask God to give us wisdom for that."

8. "I tried to be a 'scotoma buster' for my friend, but she took it the wrong way and got offended." That is a risk we take, but I also have a couple of questions for you.

   a. Have you established the type of relationship where you have acquired enough respect and mutual trust to be able to play the role of scotoma buster?

   b. Did you speak the truth in love?

   c. Choose to believe we all need scotoma busters but we have to earn the right to speak harsh truths into other people's lives.

9. "I was raised in a family that lived within defined lids and grids, and I am too afraid to try new things." God has given us unlimited resources to live an abundant life here on earth. Sometimes we need to risk new territories by stepping into our fear and seeing what is beyond our defined lids. Choose to find the kind of friend you can trust who will help you to walk through some of those fears just to see that it really is not that scary. Ask yourself, "What is the worst thing that can happen to me?"

10. "I don't know how to let go of expectations from my friends." Choose to learn that no one in this world is responsible for your happiness and well being. No matter how great a friend they are, they do not have to live up to your expectations and function the same way you would. Releasing our friends and loving them just the way they are is the best gift we can give them.

Stop and Ask God To Help You Change Sand to Pearls

Begin by asking: God, what can I do to nurture my friendships?

S Scripture: "Two are better than one, because they have a good return for their work: If one falls down, his friend can help him up. But pity the man who falls and has no one to help him up! Also, if two lie down together, they will keep warm. But how can one keep warm alone? Though one may be overpowered, two can defend themselves. A cord of three strands is not quickly broken" (Ecc. 4:9-12, NIV).

T Thanksgiving: Thank You, God, that You give us friends to help each other when we are alone and in trouble. I am so grateful for the people in my life who love me just the way I have been created. I am also grateful for the third person in my relationships: You, God. For I know that without You, I cannot overcome the possibility of being attacked, defeated and destroyed through betrayal, unfairness and unmet expectations.

O Observation: I absolutely need God as the third person in all my relationships so that when I need to forgive, God will help me. God is the only One who can heal broken hearts and severed relationships.

P Prayer: God, help me to be a good friend. I realize that I have been created for relationship, that my greatest joy comes from this wonderful concept. I must confess that sometimes I get hurt and don't believe in all its goodness. Heal my heart from expectations that have disappointed me, offended me, and where I have pulled away. I realize that relationships teach us how to live the way You designed humans to live, learning to love unconditionally. I confess I know how to do this in relationships where it is easy and fun, but I have difficulty when I need to give a mulligan and extend the gift of grace. Help my insecure heart to be strong and to learn from people who rub me the wrong way and bring out the worst in me. Teach me daily to love people just the way You created them to be, and not how I expect them to act. God, I long for a *heart song* friend, one that I know I can call at 2:00 in the morning to stand with me when I need someone to lean on. I long for the kind of friend with whom I can experience perfect moments in time, so that I can get a clearer picture of Your plan for my life, and to get glimpses of eternity. Teach me also to be a heart song friend.

Amen.

Chapter 5

Resentment or Sweet Reasonableness

The Resentment Box

Resentment is like taking poison and waiting for the other person to die.
—MALACHY MCCOURT

I call it a *resentment box*," I told the beautiful, perplexed bride. I quickly continued speaking as I had a mere seven minutes to say something profound and inspirational during my niece's wedding ceremony. The words needed to be powerful in order to get the bride and groom's attention. I saw my niece Becky out of the corner of my eye—a vision of elegant, flowing champagne silk, sparkling with sequins and crystals from the top of her exquisite head to her ballerina toes. There was a radiance about her that exuded fresh, untarnished love. She was marrying her prince charming, a dentist's son—the one with the endless smile, white teeth and gentle heart.

I knew her well and caught her puzzled, searching look. I could almost hear her thinking, *I thought I told you to speak about love—not resentment.* I dismissed the look and forged on. "It's called a resentment box because it needs to separate two love languages: the language of the lips and the language of the heart."

I continued: "The *language of the lips* is the ancient words of beautiful wedding covenant vows of love and commitment that the two of you just repeated to each other. Many of us silently wiped away tears as we heard you tenderly exchange those words of love and loyalty. We all yearn to hear words that commit to a love that is so beautiful and powerful that only death has the power to break them. Without realizing it, when we hear powerful, life-giving love language of the lips, we begin the silent language of the heart: *expectations*."

Expectations

When someone verbalizes a love so intense, pure and full of commitment, unknowingly in our mind we begin to form expectations:

- To hold hands when we walk.
- To pray together.
- He will pay the bills; I will return the movies.
- I will need to talk; he will want to listen.
- I want to go shopping; he will want to come.
- I will want to spend every Christmas with my parents; he will agree.
- He will get excited when I show him my new favorite nail polish color.

Unfortunately, life is not that predictable. We become overwhelmed with other responsibilities; we assume, forget, and didn't know. It isn't long before expectations are not met. Because we know we should love each other and be kind to each other, we paste on a nice plastic smile and we respond with our own *love language of the lips*, and we can hear ourselves say:

- "That's okay, not a problem."
- "It's fine—really."
- "Maybe next time."
- "Don't worry about it."

We can't ignore the loud beating in our chest: it is telling us something is not right. The *language of the heart* feels an undeniable twinge of pain.

Something strange is going on in there. Actions and words tell us we have been overlooked, and we are not as important and lovable as we thought. We feel hurt, angry and unloved. It's too early in the relationship to make a big scene, start a fight or let anyone see our ugly feelings. After all we are nice. So we stuff our hurt away, pretend everything is fine, and without realizing it we have built up our first *resentment* and silently tucked it away into our resentment box.

Loving relationships are meant to express and show love through encouraging words, listening by being fully engaged with our ears and eyes, by sticking up for each other when someone says something nasty, and helping each other when we feel like a failure. So each time we hear words or see actions that make us feel unloved or insignificant, there is some kind of unmet expectation. It starts with a tug at the heart—a small twinge of hurt. If we do not get an explanation, an apology or resolution, the tiny flicker of hurt bursts into a raging, uncontrollable fire. Plunk, plunk, plunk: one ugly resentment after another, into the resentment box.

One day someone innocently asks, "Did you remember to pick up milk after work?" Like a volcanic eruption the resentment box blows. Built up anger and indignation propel us to hurl accusations and itemize every hurtful word or deed that was ever done or said. Or for those that choose to deny their pain or are unwilling to clean up the mess, one day they simply pack up a suitcase and walk out of the house. Sadly, the resentment box is full and they don't have the time, energy or skills to deal with the hurt.

Resentment Is Ugly

The Random House dictionary defines resentment this way: "the feeling of displeasure or indignation at some act, remark, person, etc. regarded as causing injury or insult."[30] Synonyms for this word are: bitterness, dislike, hatred, antipathy, offense, umbrage, bile, aversion. These are menacing words of intense feelings.

It is the re-sensing of offenses, bitter emotions played over and over in our mind until they poison our lives. Because of the hurt or indignation that we have suffered, we feel justified in hoarding this resentment. We hold on to it as if it has power, like a missile to be used later. We don't realize that in the meantime, it is actually slowly poisoning and killing our soul.

Resentment is the silent, bitter *language in our heart* that burns in our soul in the middle of the night. It distorts our face with anger, makes us say ugly words and lash out with the intent to hurt someone else. If resentment it not confronted, it will make us do things we will eventually regret.

Resentment Turns to Despising

We have certain expectations when someone declares their love for us (*language of the lips*). We have certain expectations about what that will look like. We have a need to be adored and we hate being overlooked; it makes us feel worthless and insignificant. In the book of Genesis chapter 16, I believe Sarai felt overlooked by God.

God told her husband Abram, "I will make you into a great nation and I will bless you; I will make your name great, and you will be a blessing. I will bless those who bless you, and whoever curses you I will curse; and all peoples on earth will be blessed through you" (Genesis 12:2-3, NIV).

Getting older and failing to conceive, Sarai felt overlooked and forgotten by God. Where was the blessing he had promised them? Discouraged, she said to Abram, "The Lord has kept me from having children. Go, sleep with my maidservant; perhaps I can build a family through her" (Genesis 16:2, NIV).

These were the words of someone whose expectations had not been met. When resentment builds up and we take matters into our own hands, it makes us do pitiful, hurtful things.

It got worse: resentment that is not dealt with turns into despising.

Sarai gave her maidservant Hagar to Abram, and Hagar became pregnant, and the saga continued. "When she knew she was pregnant, she began to despise her mistress. Then Sarai said to Abram, 'You are responsible for the wrong I am suffering. I put my servant in your arms, and now that she knows she is pregnant, she despises me'" (Genesis 16:4-5, NIV). When events didn't turn out the way Sarai expected, she despised Hagar, and then mistreated her by sending her away into the desert.

When resentment is not dealt with, it spirals into jealousy and acts of revenge.

My Own Resentment Box

I am very familiar with the resentment box story. I was madly in love with my first husband Dick, a tall, dark and handsome basketball player. When we were married and declared our love for each other, I had romantic visions of floating through life on a cloud of happiness, of being cared for and catered to. I had *expectations*. I was too young and foolish to recognize that an expectation provides fertile ground for a predetermined resentment.

I did not know that resentment was:
- Feeling heartbroken after exerting a great deal of effort and energy to achieve something that was eventually overlooked or lost to me.
- Feeling a grudge when something was kept from me that was rightfully mine.
- Feeling that I was not heard when I expressed pain.
- Being stuck in meaningless activity.
- Accepting negative treatment and never expressing my feelings about it.
- Agreeing to do something for others yet feeling that I was being taken for granted.
- Being ignored, put down or scorned by someone for whom I made sacrifices.
- Always trying my best to please but never feeling it was good enough.
- Feeling I was making more effort and sacrifices than the other person.
- Harboring resentment toward a person or group of people whom I felt mistreated me.
- Unresolved grief when I found it difficult to accept a loss.
- Feeling hurt and suffering in silence.

Nice Girls Suffer Quietly

I had no idea I was dealing with resentment. I was raised to be a nice girl, so I kept the hurt hidden under a plastic smile and my face showed the world that life was great. Silently, the invisible razor blades were at work. They kept cutting my heart, and dark clouds of depression began haunting me, attempting to consume me. Slowly the language of my heart was killing me.

Why do we suffer silently? In her book *Tame Your Fears and Transform Them into Faith, Confidence and Action,* author Carol Kent says:

> All of us have an indescribable desire for love. We spend much of our lives trying to make relationships work so we can fill the vacuum inside our souls. For most of us, no punishment could be worse than being abandoned by someone to whom we have given our love, loyalty and commitment. But this problem goes far beyond the personal feeling of rejection we might experience. Our gripping fear is that significant other people in our lives will know we failed at the one thing Christian women are supposed to be good at—making relationships work. Especially marriage and family relationships![31]

Unresolved pain is still alive and does not simply evaporate. When we are uninformed, fearful or too nice to deal with our resentments, they will destroy our soul.

In her book *Nice Girls Don't Change the World*, Lynne Hybels tells her story of her struggles to regain the parts of her soul that she felt had been lost to her. She had to face the reality that when her heart was hurting, she had to learn to speak up. She says, "So why didn't I make the choices necessary to do that? Because nice girls just don't ask for help. They'd rather do almost anything than inconvenience other people. So they don't honor their own needs, desires, or dreams. Underneath they really don't think its okay to do that."[32]

I also felt lost, confused and helpless. One day there was no more room for another offense. Period. I was forced to look inside the box. It was uglier than I thought. I had let unmet expectations make me bitter until it was bile that I was no longer able to swallow. It was causing me to have restless and sleepless nights; I could feel irritation at the smallest inconvenience and was finding it hard to be the funny, joyful Heidi that I wanted to be.

I needed help. I am the type of person that needs to come to the end of herself before asking for help. In the Bible I found a God who is gentle and will listen to me and help me in every situation. I just need to ask Him. "If you want to know what God wants you to do, ask him, and he will gladly tell you, for he is always ready to give a bountiful supply of wisdom to all who ask him; and he will not resent it" (James 1:5, TLB).

God and I started a journey that would take years to transform my behavior. It was so much easier to blame my husband and other people in my life for not fulfilling my expectations of what I thought life should be like than it was to change myself.

Unleashing the Beauty of Sweet Reasonableness

It is hard to let go of resentment. It becomes a safe, comfortable weapon that we feel justified in holding on to. If we let it go, will we let the offenders off the hook and will we feel safe in the future?

In the book of John, chapter 5, when Jesus encounters a man who has been sick for thirty-eight years, He stops and asks him, "Do you want to get well?" (John 5:6, NIV). What a strange question. I can almost hear the whining in the man's voice when he says that he was never able to be healed because no one ever helped him. Jesus again responds in verse 8, "Get Up! Pick up your mat and walk."

I recognized my need for healing and realized that I would have to do my part. I didn't know what that would look like, but I knew where to turn.

I needed to let God do some deep, hard, penetrating soul work. I knew that God was the only one who could do this. "For the word of God is living and active. Sharper than any double-edged sword, it penetrates even to dividing soul and spirit, joints and marrow; it judges the thoughts and attitudes of the heart. Nothing in all creation is hidden from God's sight" (Hebrews 4:12-13, NIV).

Each time I felt like blaming someone for not meeting my expectations, I knew I had an opportunity to make a powerful, right choice. I had to learn to respond to each resentment by "picking up my mat" (my resentment) and beginning to learn how to exchange it for *sweet reasonableness*.

1. Choose To Accept

The first step is always the most difficult because it means that we have to stop pointing fingers and look at ourselves in the mirror. Rick Warren has a slogan: "Revealing your feeling is the beginning of healing."[33] We must stop pointing fingers of blame and admit that we have a problem. Let's ask ourselves some questions:

- Is this resentment the result of my own insecurity—never feeling good enough?
- Is this a real or imagined offense?
- What irrational thinking am I locked into because of my resentment?
- Did I just feel that I was being robbed of something valuable?
- What root of distrust or suspicion am I holding on to?
- Did I let myself be manipulated, controlled?
- What past hurt is still making me distrustful or feel abandoned and unloved?
- Why do I think that I am right?

It was time to recognize and accept that people are prone to be imperfect and make mistakes. My mistakes were that I was too proud, immature and insecure to recognize there was a problem. I had listened to the *language of my heart* that said my husband should love me in a certain way— that he would always be there for me, listen to me, support me and bring me the happiness I felt I deserved. I had placed expectations on him that he was not able to meet, and those unmet expectations turned into resentment. I was so afraid of the word "divorce" that I continued to be the nice girl and keep quiet.

2. Confront

Sometimes there is a real problem. Something must be done when we are always being mistreated, abused, put down and manipulated. Some resentments become so big that if we don't deal with them they will become huge boulders that we will throw at each other, killing the relationship. Confronting in love is hard and needs to be done lovingly and carefully, never with accusing, belittling or judging. The motive in our heart has to be pure and right, always with the intent to bring healing and love back into the relationship.

Where there is emotional abuse, we must be sure to establish strong, clear boundaries. Look to God for wisdom for the right words so that the confrontation brings healing and not more resentment.

When I first started this process with my husband, I would say to him, "Honey, there is something I have to talk to about. Something is hurting my heart and you need to hear this. I don't want you to correct me, rationalize the situation or offer immediate solutions. You need to hear what is on my heart first, without interruptions. Then I will ask for your feedback." Often I was shocked and surprised when I heard his response, realizing how irrational my resentment had been and how justified he had been in what he had done. There are always two sides to every story and the truth is somewhere in between. Before we build up resentment, it is a good idea to hear the other person's view point.

3. Know

God is the only source of our love. While we expect other people in our lives to love us and be our savior, He is the only one who can do that perfectly. We don't look to other people to fill us with love; we need to help each other to love better. The love of others is to be received and enjoyed like the beautiful, sweet icing on a wedding cake.

4. Forgive

Now that you recognize the resentment, it is time to deal with it. The only way to heal from resentment is to forgive. We must initiate the action to forgive and release the offender to God's judgment.

We are commanded to forgive others because it is the most powerful, healing decision we can make to bring us back into living a vibrant, energetic, joyful life. Forgiveness allows us to be free from the debilitating energy that is like venom surging through our veins. "Be kind and compassionate to one another, forgiving each other, just as in Christ God forgave you" (Eph. 4:32, NIV).

We may pray something like this, "God, right now, I would ask that You help me to let this go and forgive him/her for not listening to me/recognizing me/treating me with respect/showing up on time/remembering our commitment. Help me to see them through Your eyes of love, gentleness and sweet reasonableness, and give me the wisdom and power to respond in a way that will keep my heart pure and free from resentment."

If the offender has died, it is a good idea to write a letter forgiving them, and list all the details of the resentment. By taking the resentment out of the resentment box the healing has already begun. Forgiveness will clean up our resentment box and we can live in freedom and not bondage.

5. Guard

Visualize your resentment box in a shape of a heart and guard it like a prison guard. The Bible tells us how crucial this is, "Above all else, guard your heart, for it is the wellspring of life" (Proverbs 4:23, NIV).

Above all else protect your heart from resentment. Learn new behavior and attitudes and rational thinking. I need to visualize my life past, present and future without the negative impact of resentment. I must receive my self-esteem from God and not expect the people in my life to make me happy and solve my problems for me. My very best prescription for resentment is prevention. When we realize how much resentment hurts us and other people we must refuse to let it drop into our resentment box.

To guard our heart means we need to take responsibility for it. Dr. Henry Cloud says in his book, *9 Things you Simply Must* Do, "So become responsible for getting what you need and maintaining your own emotional health so that the other person cannot drag you into the gutter. If you keep your feet solidly on the high road you will be able to drag him or her up. It is like when the flight attendant tells you to first put on your own oxygen mask before helping a child put on hers. You cannot help another if you are deprived of the thing you need."[34]

It is not my job to change the world and all the people in it. My responsibility is my soul and to keep my motives and love pure. I need to focus on the future and how I can influence and love people—not expect them to influence me and be responsible for my happiness.

6. Choose Sweet Reasonableness

"Sweet reasonableness" is the poise of the soul which enables me to sacrifice my own rights out of generosity for what Christ has done for me. I believe we are afraid that if we yield to something or someone we will lose power. The opposite is true. When we yield to the godly, loving acts of forgiveness and gentleness we are free from the hooks of resentment.

The apostle Paul, formerly a violent, persecuting tyrant, demonstrated that he had learned the gentleness of God when he wrote, "Let your gentleness be evident to all" (Phil. 4:5, NIV). If the apostle Paul could exercise it, there is hope for all of us. A. W. Tozer in the book *The Best of A.W. Tozer: 52 Favorite Chapters*, says it this way: "Some of us are religiously jumpy and self-conscious because we know that God sees our every thought and is acquainted with all our ways. We need not be. God is the sum of all patience and the essence of kindly good will. We please Him most, not by frantically trying to make ourselves good, but by throwing ourselves into His arms with all our imperfections, and believing that He understands everything and loves us still."[35] *Now that is sweet reasonableness.*

When I told Becky and Grant about the resentment box story on their wedding day, I believe I gave them the best gift I could offer them for their marriage. When we recognize resentment and know how to deal with it, it keeps love and communication open. As we extend gentleness and forgiveness toward each other, we can live harmonious lives of inner peace and freedom.

God is the only one who can help us discern the *language of the lips* from the *language of the heart*, and to help us be brutally honest with ourselves when we start to see resentment build. When we learn this simple yet extremely hard process, we cannot help but stand amazed that our God can do more in our relationships than we could ever dream or imagine.

Choices That Enrich Your Life

None of us are perfect; so let's give each other some grace:

1. When there is a mother with tired, cranky children behind you in the grocery line, instead of getting irritated, choose to let her go ahead.

2. Your husband forgot to take out the garbage—again. Choose to overlook it; the world will not come to an end.

3. The restaurant is not serving the food fast enough; choose to acknowledge that the waitress may be tired and overworked.

4. Someone made an unkind remark to you at work; choose to overlook it by smiling back and complimenting them in some way.

5. Your girlfriend forgot your birthday. Choose to believe birthdays are not as important to her as they are to you.

6. You have sacrificed your time and energy for your employer for twenty years, and they forgot to honor this important milestone. Choose to realize that if you work for rewards, you set yourself up for disappointment. Obviously your employer does not consider employment recognition to be valuable. Choose to let it go and start working for God instead of man so that you "live a life worthy of the Lord and may please him in every way" (Col. 1:10, NIV).

7. Your children keep leaving their dishes on the side of the sink instead of putting them in the dishwasher. You have a choice: confront them or choose to put them into the dishwasher yourself. Do one or the other, but don't build resentment.

8. Your husband is retired but you are still working outside the home. Each day when you come home some of the chores that he promised to do are still not done. Before you start banging pots and pans, choose to find out the reason they didn't get done. Then re-negotiate and find a way to resolve this ongoing frustration. Not dealing with it will build resentment.

9. People keep doing things to annoy you. Choose to find out the cause of your frustration. Is it really them or is it you?

10. Someone in your circle of friends is always monopolizing the conversation and drawing attention to themselves. Choose to realize that they need the world to know that they also have value. Choose to feel compassion instead of annoyance.

11. When you feel angry because someone has hurt you, choose to deal with the source of that pain so that you do not build resentment.

Stop and Ask God To Help You Change Sand to Pearls

Begin by asking: God, what unresolved hurt is causing me to feel resentment?

S Scripture: "Be kind and compassionate to one another, forgiving each other, just as in Christ God forgave you" (Eph. 4:32, NIV).

T Thanksgiving: Thank You, God, that You are always kind and compassionate towards me even when I lack compassion for people in my life. Thank You for being the kindest person I have ever met. I am so grateful that You are teaching me kindness and forgiveness that unfolds into a little more sweet reasonableness each day.

O Observation: How long do I hang on to resentment before I forgive? God has commanded me to forgive so that I can exude kindness and compassion to all the people in my life. I need to ask God to help me choose sweet reasonableness over resentment every time I feel the prick of an offense.

P Prayer: God, that word "kind" quickens my heartbeat and allows me to feel Your gentleness toward me. I long for kindness from You and the people in my life—but how often do I extend it? When I experience kindness I realize it is the gentlest expression of love and we all yearn to receive more and more of it. God, You have taught me about resentment and I realize that I have a responsibility to keep my heart pure. I know that every time I feel resentment dropping into the resentment box I have to choose to forgive. Teach me and remind me over and over again that this is not an option and that instead of building up resentment, I need to choose gentleness and forgiveness, which are the ingredients of sweet reasonableness.

Thank You that You are patient and kind toward me and that You continue to prompt me when I slide back into old habits. I know that when I make the powerful choice to be kind and forgive, I live a life full of freedom and joy. Quicken my heart and prompt me with Your Holy Spirit when I begin to harbor resentment and give me the wisdom and power to be kind and make wise and good choices every day. Thank You.

Amen.

Chapter 6

Broken or Blended

Can We Still Go Through the Cupboards?

All happy families are alike, but an unhappy family
is unhappy after its own fashion.

—LEO TOLSTOY, *Anna Karenina*, 1877

My body was ice cold and shivering as I sat huddled with my arms wrapped around my legs. Tears streamed down my face and my mind whirled with confusion and indecision, as the rain mercilessly continued to pelt onto the tile roof of the little church on the Rock of Gibraltar.

It was the day before New Year's Eve, and I was in southern Spain with my two children Michelle and Donovan, my son-in-law Tim, my son's girl-friend Brenda and my new fiancé-to-be—Jack. After the death of my first husband, it was time to embrace my new life. I had fallen in love with an amazing man and we planned our engagement to take place on New Year's Eve in beautiful Marbella, Spain.

This process had started months before when my daughter Michelle sat across from me in a coffee shop and gently said, "Mom, I have noticed that you and Jack love spending time together. We all thought it might be nice if you brought him along on our family trip to Spain." I knew this was a sacrificial decision for my children; I was amazed that they were willing to forfeit their comfort so I could begin to enjoy life again.

The reality of telling my children about the upcoming engagement left me paralyzed with questions. How would they react? Why had I not prepared them more? Was I ready to become the mother of five children? How would this affect my relationship with my own children? Did I even want to get married just as I was beginning to enjoy my single life? The haunting questions kept spiraling without me finding any constructive answers.

Without realizing it, I had been gone for hours and everyone was frantically looking for me. It was Jack who finally found me. He was perplexed when he saw me sitting there, drenched and cold. He knew there was trouble when he saw my trembling body and the agony and terror in my eyes. I didn't even want to look at his bewildered face as I poured out all my uncertainties and endless questions. His head hung as he listened, and after a long silence he quietly said, "Whatever you decide, that is what I will honor." I wasn't prepared for such compassion and kindness; but those words melted my heart. Almost immediately my body stopped shaking and for the first time that day, I felt resolved and at peace. I believed that a man who was willing to sacrifice his own desires would love me enough to help me through the difficult times and adjustments that lay ahead. A calming resolution flowed through me; my decision was made. There was no doubt that this was the man I wanted to marry.

We ran through the assaulting rain to the restaurant where my family was anxiously waiting for me. Before I lost my nerve I quickly informed them that I had some very important news to tell them. Their bewildered and confused faces stared at me when I blurted out, "Jack and I are planning to be engaged tomorrow night, and we hope that we have your blessing."

I knew they would be surprised, but I was not prepared for the shock and disbelief in their eyes. The girls started to cry and we left the restaurant to start the long, awkward, silent ride back to the condominium. When we arrived we separated and everyone solemnly slipped into their own beds. Eventually I fell into a restless sleep. At 2:00 in the morning, there was a knock on the door, and my daughter whispered, "Mom, please come downstairs. We all want to talk to you."

There was my family sitting in a circle in the living room, looking at me with bewildered and tear-stained faces. While I was tossing and turning in my bed, they had been sitting here for hours trying to come to terms with what they heard that night. I had taught my children to talk to me about everything that was difficult for them, to communicate honestly about what was troubling them. No matter how bad it was, I always reassured them that we could work it out. Now they needed the same honesty from me, and I was on the hot seat. I was grateful that I had a family that loved me enough to overcome their tiredness, the emotional awkwardness, the pain and misery to begin a very necessary, urgent and emotionally fragile talk. They challenged me with the fact that the engagement was all too much, way too soon, too fast. They still needed time to grieve their father. My children told me frankly that they simply were not ready for the next phase of my life. For the rest of the night we questioned each other: When does grieving end? What is the right time to remarry? Is there ever a good and right time for anything? How did they fit into this new picture? How would we move forward from here?

Finally the morning sun broke the heavy darkness and we knew we had to start a new day. Slowly and painfully we wiped away our tears, hugged and slipped off to bed to salvage a few more hours of sleep.

For my family it was important to communicate with gut-level honesty to prevent anger and conflict. So far it had brought us through many difficult times and always allowed us to move forward with a determined, positive and refreshed focus. Now the question lingered in the air unanswered. How would we unleash the next phase of our life as a blended family?

I don't have the magical formula for blending two families successfully; all I know is the journey our two families took. The preparation for combining two families is not a ten- or twelve-step program. There is often unresolved pain, confusion and many times hostility and unforgiveness. I believe that for most people when there is a change in family dynamics, there is an undetected question that lingers and begs to cry out: "Will I still feel loved?"

Defining the "Very Good" Grid

Jack and I had learned enough in our first marriages to know that there are several ingredients needed to establish the kind of marriage that was designed by God. We both believed that everything God has made is *very good*, "God saw all that he had made, and it was very good" (Genesis 1:31, NIV). Jack and I both knew we wanted a *very good marriage*.

We were now old enough, and had experienced enough emotions, to know that "being in love" releases pleasure chemicals in our brains that give us a false feeling of what love actually is. Although that is a gorgeous feeling we want to hang on to forever, we know that when unwelcome trouble and trials come knocking at our door, this feeling begins to disappear and we wonder if we have actually "fallen out of love." We had both been married long enough to discover that people don't just fall in and out of love. We firmly believed that love is from God; it is a fruit of the Holy Spirit that needs to be nurtured.

Bob and Audrey Meisner experienced what it feels like when our natural feelings of love and affection run out when one of them ended up in an affair. They explain this in their brutally authentic book, *Marriage Undercover*. They wrote, "The day came when our natural love and affection ran out. That's when we had to learn what true love was really all about. It wasn't about roles or expectations of being a "good" husband or a "good" wife or raising a "good" family or just getting along together; all of those are possible in the natural. It was when we faced a crisis that nearly tore us apart that we learned that we needed a love that was beyond ourselves, a supernatural love, a love that finds both its source and its fulfillment in God, a love that is eternal and can face any threat and overcome any obstacle."[36]

We wanted to make sure we both understood this supernatural love that needed to endure many difficult obstacles and challenges.

Designing the Plan

God has given all of us different personalities, gifts and interests; and there is incredible joy and freedom when we allow each other to be who God created us to be. In a marriage we can give each other that freedom and permission if both people share common core values. Jack and I wanted to see what our core values were. Without any coaching or discussion, we decided to write our individual core values in the form of a mission statement. When we compared our notes, we were delighted and amazed. Of course our wording was completely different because we have unique personalities, but our goals and values were unified. We spent hours combining our words and preparing them to be our life's mission statement. This is what it looked like on the back of our wedding bulletin. Today this mission statement is framed and sits on a table in our foyer.

Our Mission Statement:

We desire first of all, to know and
understand God intimately. And
allow the Father's love to
transform us into the people that
He has destined us to be.

We solemnly covenant to love and
encourage each other in order
that the gifting and abilities that
God has given us would come into
complete fruition.

We will endeavour to extend the
unconditional love we have
received from God to our families,
supporting and encouraging them
in any given situation.

> Finally, it is our heart's desire to
> impart the Father's love through
> word and deed to all of those
> whom God places in our lives,
> knowing that the love which we
> have received is one of the most
> precious gifts that we can give to others.
>
> JACK AND HEIDI MCLAUGHLIN

Looks Good, But How Does It Work?

1. Choose To Nurture Your Own Soul

I went into my first marriage as a young, insecure nineteen-year-old, expecting my husband to love me, fulfill all my desires and complete me a woman. I was in for the painful discovery that he was expecting the same thing from me. We were not wise or strong enough to meet each other's needs and it caused a lot of power struggles, unnecessary arguments, wasted energy and lots of pain. *Two broken people cannot produce a whole marriage. Period.*

Jack and I both knew it was our individual responsibility to nurture our own souls so that we did not look to each other to meet all our emotional and spiritual needs. God is the only one who can heal our brokenness and transform us into the people we were designed to be. When we come into a relationship as whole, confident, secure people, we have the ability to *pour love* onto each other with joy and freedom and not try to *pull love* out of each other. Love flows through us from God, our Creator, and is completed and made even more beautiful when we become love dispensers—not love quenchers.

In Gary Thomas' book, *Sacred Influence*, makes this more clear, "While some women define themselves on the basis of how one man (or men in general) views them and accepts them, as a *Christian* woman you have the opportunity to define yourself in relation to your creator—not in defiance to your husband but in a way that will complement your marriage and bless your husband."[37] He goes on to say, "Your husband cannot possibly be all things that you need for your own personal development—and emotional and spiritual health—outside the marriage".[38]

God is the one who created us: He is the only one who knows us inside and out and can bring us into our destiny. We cannot expect our husbands to meet all those empty places in our hearts. In order to make a marriage thrive, we have to be healed and thrive as an individual first.

2. Choose To Love and Encourage Each Other

When we are confident in who we are it is much easier to offer encouragement to others, and to not always selfishly draw attention to ourselves. When we feel secure we don't need constant approval and are delighted when other people succeed. Jack and I made a covenant that we would help each other to unleash our gifts, achieve our dreams, and to allow each other the grace to make mistakes on this journey of discovery. We both wanted to see the potential of what God could do in our lives as individuals, and as a couple.

We agreed with the apostle Paul when he wrote, "Do nothing out of selfish ambition or vain conceit, but in humility consider others better than yourselves. Each of you should look not only to your own interests, but also to the interests of others" (Phil. 2:3-4, NIV).

This is much easier to read than to do because humanly speaking, we are all quite needy and selfish. But by focusing on the other person's interests, we have watched as God has unleashed some of our goals, dreams and desires. When I had a dream of writing my first book, Jack unselfishly was my greatest encourager and supporter. We spent hours at our kitchen counter or sitting on our patio deck as he listened to my endless ramblings, stories and ideas. He challenged and questioned me, but never gave useless criticism or tried to squelch my spirit. Instead he helped me refocus with fresh perspective. He supports my speaking and traveling and prays for me when I leave, and throughout the times I speak I get regular text messages saying, "How are you doing? I'm praying for you!"

3. Choose Respect

I believe it is important that we be confident enough to follow the instruction of the apostle Paul when he speaks to the wives: "... and the wife must respect her husband" (Eph. 5:33, NIV).

The author Shaunti Feldhan did a ground breaking nationwide survey and personal interviews of more than 1,000 men, and then wrote the book and Bible study called *For Women Only*. In the Bible study she makes the bold statement: "A man's greatest need is to feel respected."[39] She goes on to say, "Of course, your love is, and will always be important, but, the man in your life may need your respect as much as, if not more than, your love."[40]

I was so fascinated with her book that I formed several groups of women to study this material. Each time we came to the subject of respect, it opened a floodgate of discussion. First of all, most women don't know that this is the number one need for all men, and secondly, many women feel that many men don't deserve to be treated with respect. We had to come to the ultimate decision that it is not about *deserving* but about being *obedient* to how God wants us to treat each other.

I have watched how God unfolds this in relationships, and I have discovered this to be absolutely true. I know my husband needs my respect, and at this stage in my life I feel confident enough to give it to him. I also offer my support by telling him how much I respect him when he speaks, preaches or leads a Bible study. I affirm him for his spiritual disciplines, his regular workout programs at the gym and the use of his spiritual gifts. God has given him different gifts than me, but I encourage him and tell him how much I respect him for shoveling our neighbor's driveways, visiting sick people, being a good listener and being the last one out of the door when there is a task to be done. I believe that a goal and value for a wife is to show her husband respect. There will be situations and times when we feel that our husbands have not earned the right to our respect, but as a response to God's command, we need to choose to respect our husbands by the way we treat them or speak to them.

Out of that obedience, I believe we will begin to see life-transforming evidence as our men begin to respond by treating us as the most wonderful women in the world. If you have lost respect for them because they are involved in something immoral or illegal, however, that is a completely different matter and you need to seek wise counsel. Gary Thomas goes on say this about respect, "Without feeling appreciated, admired and genuinely respected, your husband probably will never change."[41] When we choose to respect our husbands, it is our most powerful and intimate way of telling them, "I love you."

4. Choose Love

Men need our respect—we need love. The Bible commands this, "Husbands, love your wives, just as Christ loved the church and gave himself up for her" (Eph. 5:25, NIV).

God made women to be beautiful, emotional creatures and our deepest need is to be loved. One of the greatest love gifts a man can give a woman is to listen to her. I know that it is hard for many men to sit and listen to the emotional ramblings of a woman. I also know that men have a difficult time watching a woman cry, because men need to know how to fix something, and they don't know how to fix tears. But when they grasp the concept of choosing to listen to the mysteries in our hearts, we will feel validated and loved. A note of caution for all of us women: don't abuse this with constant drama, tears and endless chatter; most men simply don't know how to deal with that.

Fortunately Jack has grasped this incredible knowledge of listening, and he shows his love to me by listening to my discussions of how I see situations and perceive people, making it possible for me to unload the frustrations and share the joys of everyday living.

Men need to tap into their wife's love language. When they begin to understand that their wife feels loved when she is listened to, has been given help with the laundry, or has been given a romantic dinner or gift, a magical transformation will begin to take place. A note to any man reading this book: Women are not that hard to please; show them evidence of your love and kindness, and they will probably never leave you.

5. Choose To Blend

When we become strong and healthy as individuals, then we are ready to incorporate other people into our lives in a constructive manner. Jack and my blending started long before the wedding.

    a. Jack and I organized our own "business lunches" where we exposed our bills, arranged our finances, set up separate and combined bank accounts and credit cards. We also coordinated our health insurance, set limits on our gift spending and decided how we would handle Christmas presents. Because there were two estates involved, we clearly defined who would pay for what. Looking back, I see that this as an incredibly wise and crucial step to eliminating ugly surprises that have the potential to surface after the marriage vows are said.

    b. We wanted our children to feel safe and secure, so we sat them down and explained how the estate money would flow after we were deceased. We wanted them to be assured that what belonged to them would always belong to them. They needed to be clear and understand that even though our family dynamics were changing, our love and care for them would never change.

    c. Two of our girls made this same comment on two separate occasions: "After you and Jack get married, will we still be able to go through the cupboards?" That disguised question revealed the true nature of their uncertainties. They needed to know that after Jack and I were married, *would their home be the safe and comfortable place they always knew it to be and would they still feel loved?* That was a defining inquiry for us, and Jack and I went to work to create a unique home for all of them; a place where they would know they were loved and belonged.

        We sold both our homes and had a new one built to accommodate our new large family. I realize that everyone is at a different stage in their life and not able to orchestrate their plans this way, but I think that when we are blending families, it is important to start the new family on neutral ground. I don't think either family wants to be saturated by the other family's history, furniture and stuff. I don't think we want our children comparing who has more ownership in the new territory.

In our new home we created two special bedrooms. My children's room was called the "Conley Room" and it had all the drapes, bedspreads, books and pictures from my other home. The other room was named the "McLaughlin Room" and it represented McLaughlin furniture, photo albums, memorabilia, pictures and even hand towels. These spaces were designed so that whenever a child came home from either side of the family, they would always be able to go into a room that was familiar, comfortable and held memories from a previous life that had been the most defining part of their life.

Even if you are not able to have separate bedrooms, there is always a way to prepare a sleeping area for a child that makes him or her feel that they belong. They need to know that this is their home, a place where they are loved and feel safe.

Then we built a "Heritage Wall." This was a wall in our large family room where we used an entire wall to create a picture history of both families. We wanted every child or grandchild to come into that area to grasp their roots, and see evidence of all the people in their lives who had shaped their character. As our children marry and have more children, we keep adding to this wall. It is a tangible display of all the people who have built significant value in all our lives

Simple, Everyday Values

It is never too late to start making your home a tangible expression of your desire to blend your families. There are small, yet significant everyday

things we can all do to make our homes a haven of love and joy instead of
conflict.

- Laughter is one of the greatest gifts we can give each other. Laughter covers wounds and causes us to forget trivial offenses. Choose to find ways to make your family laugh.
- Family meal times are a magical, powerful way to bring families closer together. When we take the time to slow down, connect with each other and actually talk to each other, it will build bridges instead of making children feeling unloved or abandoned. A great way to start a conversation around the table is to ask: "What was the best part of your day?"
- Get into that family closet and bring out the board games or puzzles. At first you might hear some groans, but games have the potential to bring more healing than weeks of counseling.
- Everyone can take the time to stop at an ice cream shop, take a walk and talk about the difficulties of the day.
- Turn off that TV and get everyone away from their computers or technical devices—at least for a short period of time. There is no better way to blend relationships than to spend valuable time together.
- Walk the dog—together.
- Take the children on overnight excursions on an individual basis. Get to really know them, their hurts and desires. When we know someone is really listening to us, we will feel valued.
- Show up when someone is hurting and needs to talk. Just be there!

We worked very hard at making our home a place of love and laughter. I confidently say that all our children love to come home. During the Christmas season of 2008 we had fifteen children and grandchildren home for the holidays. There were mattresses on the floor, toys scattered everywhere, and towels and clothes flung over lampshades. The kitchen was full of cooks always in the midst of preparing another meal. But our house was filled with endless activity and laughter.

Two of the Hardest Things

1. No Unrealistic Expectations

Whether we are blending a family after a divorce or death, the dynamics may be different but the principles are the same. No matter what situation we are in, the hardest decision we have to make is that we *must choose to accept each other the way we are.* The Bible shows exactly how this works where it reads, "Accept one another, then, just as Christ accepted you, in order to bring praise to God" (Rom. 15:7, NIV).

This may be easy to read and say—but very difficult to accomplish. We all have a visual picture of how we want something to look; how we want people to act. Everyone involved in blending a family sees the world through a different pair of lenses, and in their mind creates an image and has expectations of what this new family will look like.

Most people coming together in a blended family are probably still dealing with their own grief, anger and perhaps unforgivenesss. They may be looking to you to be the savior of their pain, or they expect to have nothing to do with you. Either way, these expectations are the obstacle which infuses more pain and failure because no one can live up to everyone's expectations.

Unrealized expectations cause further hurt and anger. How often do we hear?
- "I thought she would have... "
- "I can't believe they didn't... "
- "Can you believe they never... "
- "I wish they would stop... "
- "I hope they will start... "

If we don't die to our unrealistic expectations, we will constantly be at war with someone in our mind and continue to harbor resentment and unforgiveness. We cannot expect other people to fulfill our hopes and dreams of our imagined ideal life.

2. Accepting Each Other, Faults and All

We need to work hard at putting into practice this command, "Be kind and compassionate to one another, forgiving each other, just as in Christ God forgave you" (Eph. 4:32, NIV). There is incredible freedom and peace in a family when we let go of expectations and begin to accept and forgive each other, faults and all.

I never wanted to place unrealistic expectations on my new stepchildren and I hope and pray that I accomplished this. I choose to love and accept them exactly how they are at this very moment; there is nothing I can do to change them. I know that I need to accept them in the same way that Christ has accepted me—with all my sins, faults and failures.

As a mother and stepmother of a blended family, I can write with all honesty that I have been showered with a wealth of love and blessing from my new family. My stepdaughter Janice expressed this to me in a very tangible and unique way.

Jack and I were visiting Ken, Janice and our grandsons Brendon, Alex and Ryan, who live on Vancouver Island, in a distinctive home overlooking the picturesque Georgia Strait. After a noisy, laughter-filled supper hour Janice and I went for a walk along the ocean. We were deep in tender and intimate conversation about her mother, who had died of cancer. We talked about death, but also about new life and hope that people bring us. At one point she stopped and looked me in the eyes and said, "Heidi, I have learned to love you so much; can I call you mother"? I was startled because I never *expected* to hear those words—but overjoyed because I did. I embraced her and replied, "I would be so honored if you would call me mom." Between lapses of gentle silence and moments of chatter, our steps slowly took us back to the house and reality; but I know our hearts were still warm from what we had just experienced.

Time passed and Janice kept asking me questions: What colors did I love; what were my favorite fabrics; what kind of designs did I love? I knew she was up to something! Two years later there was a box underneath the Christmas tree and I was eager with anticipation. On Christmas morning

I unwrapped the mysterious box and unfolded the most magnificent hand-made quilt I have ever seen. Raspberry-colored silk with handmade rosettes covered this stunning piece of art. To me this was not just a quilt; it was a tangible expression of a labor of love. A visible object that said, "I accept you as my mom, and I love you."

Prayer Is the Power That Blends

After Jack and I were married for a year, the stark reality hit me that I was indeed the mother, stepmother and grandmother of a large family. All our children live in different places in Western Canada and the northern United States, and at times it felt like we were all so disconnected. I suggested to Jack that we needed to spend regular time together each morning to pray for our family. With that many active, energetic, busy people in our family, there was always something that we needed to pray about. Even if we could not be there with our children, we could connect with them in spirit and pray that God would guide and protect them through our prayers.

We call them our "Prayer Chairs" and we continue to meet each day to pray for our families, along with other needs in our daily lives. Our children know that we meet there, and often the phone will ring early in the morning, "Dad, can you pray for Alex? He has strep throat," or, "Mya is running a fever," or someone is having trouble in school, or there is trouble in someone's workplace, or.... In a large family, the needs are endless—but there is always the power of God to see us through those troubled times. Through the power of our Almighty God, who is close to all of us, He can unite us in spirit and bring peace, truth and wisdom into our lives through prayer.

... Or Broken

We always have the power of choice. We can choose not to belong to a new family by nurturing resentment and anger about unwanted circumstances. We can also choose to foster unrealistic expectations and when those are not met we can confidently say, "See, I told you this wouldn't work." Or, "I just don't feel accepted and loved."

Whenever dynamics change in relationships, from divorce or death, there will be pain. I never want to make light of this; it is not easy. Especially the children suffer when they are unable to deal with the change or cannot let go of their grief and pain. Bob and Audrey Meisner address this: "How does the devil destroy families? Often, he sets up young children to have hardened hearts, unable to share who they are."[42]

When my children got me out of my bed in the middle of the night to confront me about my engagement to Jack, they may not have realized it, but they opened the door to healing. Communication and honesty are two great building blocks for beginning to blend a family. When we make ourselves vulnerable enough to say, "I am still angry and hurting," we can find ways to help each other.

All of us make horrible mistakes in our lives. Let's not ruin our tomorrows by beating ourselves up with the reminder of our mistakes and being mired in regrets. The good news is we can start making better choices starting today. Even if you completely messed up trying to blend your new family, today is a good day to start incorporating some ideas and values that will bring restoration and change.

In a blended family there has been much pain, and everyone is probably wondering if they are loved and if they belong. I gave you examples of how we tried to be creative to make it work for our family. Every family has different values and dynamics, but everyone has the creativity and ability to create a place of love and acceptance. God is the one who restores our pain and gives us a new heart and new opportunities. We need God's wisdom in learning how to create and restore a place of love and belonging in our physical living spaces so that we live as families that are blended and not broken.

Choices That Enrich Your Life

1. You feel abandoned. Choose to believe you have not been abandoned, you just feel that way. Choose to find the truth. Even if you believe that your family has abandoned you, God will never

abandon you. Jesus himself said, "I will not leave you as orphans; I will come to you" (John 14:18, NIV).

2. You are still grieving for the way life used to be. Choose to be honest with your feelings and tell someone, so that they can help you with your grief.

3. You don't like your new stepmother/stepfather. Choose to give it time and begin to look for good qualities. Everyone has something good about them.

4. You feel torn between families because of a divorce. Choose to talk openly about your confusion so that your new parents can help you find closure.

5. You're not sure why or how, but you feel guilty about the break-up of your family. Choose to find truth about the guilt by going to counseling or speaking to a trusted friend.

6. The TV show *The Brady Bunch* was a lie. It has led us to believe that blending two families is an easy, fun and smooth process. It isn't.[43] Choose to overlook the sitcom fantasy and recognize that it will take work and effort.

7. You don't feel a part of this family. Choose to make an effort to become a part of it. Repeatedly tell yourself that one day you will be a part of this family—it takes time.

8. You are still angry about the divorce. Choose to believe that anger will only destroy you and make you lose sleep and waste energy. Find someone to walk you through that anger and find healing.

9. Everyone has irritating habits. You have three choices on how to deal with things that bug you about your new family members. Confront them, bury them and build resentment or get over it.

10. You hate your new home. Choose to make an effort to create an area of familiarity and comfort in your own personal area of the house.

11. You didn't get invited to your new family for Thanksgiving/Christmas. Choose to find out what happened. Did everyone get invited and you were left out, or was it an open invitation, or did everyone

else invite themselves? Before you let hurt fester into resentment, choose to find the truth.

12. A family reunion is coming up and there is unresolved history of hurt and pain with some people in the family. Choose to forgive and surrender your hurt to God. God will help you to be "more than a conqueror" of your anguish. "No, in all these things we are more than conquerors through him who loved us" (Rom. 8:37, NIV).

13. Choose to forgive, forgive, forgive.

Stop and Ask God To Help You Change Sand to Pearls

Begin by asking: God, have I placed unrealistic expectations on anyone?

S Scripture: "Accept one another, then, just as Christ accepted you, in order to bring praise to God" (Rom. 15:7, NIV).

T Thanksgiving: Thank You, God that You accept me just the way I am. I realize I am far from perfect and even though I try to hide my faults and sins, I know You see right through me. Yet You always forgive me. Thank You that You will provide me the power to accept people in my life in the same way.

O Observation: I hate to admit it, but when I don't accept other people, I am demonstrating that I think I am better than them. Forgive me for thinking that. We are all Your creatures, God, and we all have our own pain and struggles. By accepting my difficult circumstances, I see that I am bringing praise to You, God.

P Prayer: God, I get discouraged when things in life don't work out the way I anticipate. I feel hurt when people let me down and my hurt sometimes turns into anger and unforgiveness. God, You are the only one who can turn my pain and sorrow into peace and freedom. I choose to look up to You and praise You, so that my eyes and heart will be focused on You and all Your goodness and power, instead of my circumstances, which sometimes cause me sorrow and grief.

God, help me to keep focusing on You—the source of all my expectations that are good and true. Sometimes I feel that the world's promises are vain and empty. Your words and promises are truth. You are God: You do not lie. Lord, when life gets tough and people let me down, I pray that I will remember to cling to You and Your promises. Thank You that You never abandon, overlook or reject me. Thank You that You are a safe place I can run to any time of the day or night. Thank You.

Amen.

Chapter 7

Instant Pleasures or Expectant Waiting

Buyer's Remorse and Pleasure Hangovers

*Freedom of choice is more to be treasured
than any possession earth can give.*

—DAVID O. MCKAY

*W*e would like to return the car; we made a hasty decision and have decided we can't afford it." I can always tell when someone has been awake all night—tormented and agonizing over the purchase of their new car. Their eyes are red-rimmed, downcast, and their faces white and tense from lack of sleep. A car purchase that started out as a thrill became a truth of horror when the huge monthly payments became a cruel reality. Now all they want is to get rid of this ugly, tormenting burden.

Some of our instant pleasures are even more of a yoke and not that easy to get rid of.

During the early years of my first marriage I had a girlfriend who loved horses. She and I borrowed or rented horses and rode through the beautiful, endless sage mesas, mountains and fields in and around where

I lived: Penticton, British Columbia. I fell in love with horses and discovered the freedom of riding bareback with my hair blowing in the wind and the sun hitting my cheeks. What incredible liberty and enjoyment to feel the power and rhythm of the horse taking me through meadows, trails and canyons. All I could talk about was having my own horse, and my husband Dick wanted to help me gratify this new desire. One morning I went out into our back yard and tethered to a tree was a gorgeous, gentle-looking palomino. My very own horse and she was so beautiful I called her "Misty." I could hardly believe that my wish had come true, and that I could now have all the delight I wanted with this horse; every day, any time, without limits.

Within the hour I realized that horses need a home, they need to be fed and I didn't even know where to start. This new pleasure quickly turned into an inconvenience beyond anything I could have conceived. Eventually I found a shelter for Misty, at an outrageous monthly fee that would stretch our already meager finances. Then of course she had to be fed every day, which meant finding a supply of food, having it delivered and driving miles each day to feed her and spend time brushing her beautiful, golden mane. Now that I had my own horse I felt that I had to ride her every weekend. Adding to all those extra responsibilities was the cost of a saddle, having her shoed, medicine, ointments and cleaning out her stall. The amusement swiftly turned into daily drudgery and all I wanted was to be rid of these extra duties. Within months I became pregnant with my daughter Michelle, and it gave me a reasonable excuse to sell the horse. After all, how could I look after a horse and a new baby? What a relief when I found a buyer and I waved good-bye as I watched my Misty leaving in the back of a horse trailer.

I am sure we all have a story of an incident when we desperately wanted something, thought we needed to have it, and were sure it would change our lives and bring us endless satisfaction. What a shocking reality when the thrill wore off and the monthly payments started or the first dent, stain or rip caused it to lose all its appeal.

God Created Us for Pleasure

We all love to feel good and are looking for the stimulation that will give us an adrenaline rush of pleasure. God created us to enjoy that exquisite feeling.

We are created in the image of the God who created heaven, earth and all the planets and stars in this gorgeous, vast universe. He created us so that He could love on us and enjoy His relationship with us. He created us for His pleasure.

"In love he predestined us to be adopted as his sons through Jesus Christ, in accordance with his pleasure and will" (Eph. 1:4-5, NIV).

God doesn't give us these feelings of pleasure to drive us crazy yearning for things we can't have. God had big dreams for His pleasure when He created our planet, and I believe He has put big dreams of pleasure in our hearts that allow us to live an abundant life and bring us incredible fulfillment.

In his book *The Purpose-Driven Life*, Rick Warren agrees with this. He says, "One of the greatest gifts God has given you is the ability to enjoy pleasure. He wired you with five senses and emotions so you can experience it. He wants you to enjoy life, not just endure it. The reason you are able to enjoy pleasure is that God made you *in his image*."[44]

Those five senses have been given to us to enjoy. Think about how you feel when you:

- Look at a newborn baby.
- Stroke a puppy or kitten.
- Watch a bride walk down the aisle.
- Sing along to your favorite song.
- Behold moonbeams dancing on the water.
- Watch your football team win a championship game.
- View a sun setting in a blaze of color over the horizon.
- Comfort a grieving friend.
- Laugh outrageously.
- Hear someone tell you they love you.
- Cook a new, delicious recipe.

Our Pleasure Hub

Everything God gives us is to enhance our life and help us. When we overuse or abuse the good things God has given us, it can harm or even destroy us.

Somehow we have gotten off-track and have become selfishly consumed with finding pleasures for ourselves in anything that will give us that delicious, addictive rush. We will do almost anything to have it. A flash of pleasure feels like a drug, because in fact it is. As shocking as it sounds, our brains have been created to release drugs that are as powerful as heroin. This is all documented in great detail in Daniel Goleman's book, *Social Intelligence,* where he states: "Spindle cells are rich in receptors for serotonin, dopamine and vasopressin. These brain chemicals play key roles in bonding with others, in love, in our moods good and bad, and in pleasure."[45] He goes on to say, "Decades after Bowlby and Ainsworth proposed their theories, neuroscientists identified two pleasure-inducing neurotransmitters, oxytocin and endorphins, that are activated by looping. Oxytocin generates a satisfying relaxation; endorphins mimic the addictive pleasure of heroin in the brain (though not nearly so intensely)."[46]

God created our brains to have a pleasure hub, which would allow us to experience the incredible joy of knowing Him, His creation and all the things He has placed at our disposal. Sadly, we have become selfish, wiley and manipulative and have found avenues for constantly feeding this hedonistic pleasure system. We have become rats on a wheel demanding more and more effort to keep us happy.

In his book, *Thrilled to Death,* Dr. Archibald D. Hart writes extensively on how our overindulgence in pleasure numbs our brain. He says, "According to several researchers, modern humans have to keep running after things that make us feel better—success, achievements, addictions, and all that we can consume. This process is accurately called the *hedonic treadmill* by those scientists who study happiness."[47] He goes on to explain a new clinical term called "anhedonia—a feeling of joylessness and cheerlessness. It is a phenomenon that is growing in leaps and bounds. Scientists are adamant that as we push the stress level and exciting stimulation higher and higher, we are literally overloading the pathways to the pleasure center of the brain."[48]

As I observe the world around me—my workplace, my children, grand-children and my church—I see daily affirmations of all of us on that hedonic treadmill.

Instant Pleasure

Each one of us has found an avenue for getting pleasure, because we feel we need it to keep enjoying life here on earth. Life without feeling good is dull, lethargic, not creative, disappointing, and depressing. Over the last dozen years our pursuit of pleasure has escalated at a disturbing rate. Everywhere we look we are lured into thinking that we are entitled to instant bliss; and there is always a way to get it.

I have started a file with brochures and advertising that comes through the mail. Some of it says:

- What are you dreaming of? Get what you want sooner.
- You've been pre-approved for $50,000.00.
- There is something for everyone—and a lot for you.
- No matter where you dream of going, this credit card can get you there faster.
- The no-hassle way to pay.
- Everyone wins.

I believe these hooks and enticements for instant indulgence are part of the cause of the economic crisis that we are experiencing today. Through media and other people, we have been brainwashed to believe that we *deserve to have whatever we want today—don't worry about tomorrow*. However, tomorrow does come and the harsh reality wakes us up. The payments have to be made; and we have to get up in the morning to go back to work or get the money some other way. There is always a deferred payment for instant pleasure that has no lasting value, and we experience it as a "pleasure hangover."

Pleasure for stuff is one thing, but it gets even worse when it involves injecting drugs into our bodies, mutilating or cutting our bodies, or having illicit sexual relationships. They will destroy our soul, tear apart relationships and devastate our families.

I believe we are living in very disturbing times where our constant indulgences have swirled out of control. It is a real wakeup call for me when I am warned in a book that was written over 2,000 years ago: "But mark this: There will be terrible times in the last days. People will be lovers of themselves, lovers of money, boastful, proud, abusive, disobedient to their parents, ungrateful, unholy, without love, unforgiving, slanderous, without self-control, brutal, not lovers of the good, treacherous, rash, conceited *lovers of pleasure rather than lovers of God*—having a form of godliness but denying its power" (2 Tim. 3:1-5, NIV, italics mine).

There is a huge price to pay when we are "lovers of things" that violate our boundaries, compromise our souls and have the potential to hurt another human being. This is not a twenty-first-century struggle; we have been compelled to find pleasure since the beginning of time.

We've talked about Adam and Eve choosing pleasure over obedience by eating the forbidden fruit. I believe this started us down the wrong path of the pursuit of wanting whatever gives us instant gratification. Unfortunately, the consequences of these choices spiral into pain and remorse.

There are more stories:

- King David saw something he wanted and went after it. "From the roof he saw a woman bathing. The woman was very beautiful, and David sent someone to find out about her" (2 Sam. 11:2-3, NIV). He slept with her, she got pregnant, and to protect himself, he had her husband Uriah killed. Then we read, "But the thing David had done displeased the Lord" (2 Sam. 11:27, NIV). Turmoil was the heading of the next chapter for this family. The baby died and God said that murder would be a constant threat in his family. The consequence of David's poor choice cost many lives.
- Amnon, son of David, fell in love with his sister Tamar and wanted her so badly that he raped her. Immediately after he had gratified his desire the remorse set in and his feelings changed toward her.

"Then Amnon hated her with intense hatred. In fact, he hated her more than he had loved her. Amnon said to her, 'Get up and get out!'" (2 Sam. 13:15, NIV). His brother Absalom ended up killing him and it says that Tamar ended up living a life of "a desolate woman" (2 Sam. 13:20, NIV). Amnon's choice for instant gratification cost him his own life. His powerful desire caused his sister to live a desolate life.

We've been struggling with the fulfillment of our desires from the beginning of time. Apparently it is getting worse and we are abusing our insatiable desires to the point of numbing our pleasure systems.

Pleasure Overload

We are caught up in a culture where we are overloading our pleasure system with cell phones in one ear, iPods in the other, one hand on the keyboard of our computer answering e-mails and the other hand text messaging. Our movies are pushing the edge in all areas of stimulation with explicit sex scenes, violence, swirling lights and movement—louder, faster! We are afraid to let our children watch a PG movie because we're not sure it is without sex and violence.

I have nine grandchildren and I marvel at the simplicity of the joy that I see in their discovery of the world when they are still very young. They burst into a smile simply by seeing the smile on their mom or dad's face. A bird's feather has the ability to make them stop and laugh. They delight over a colored rock, butterfly, dandelion or an airplane flying overhead. Their pleasure system for enjoying the simple things in life and their ability to create has not yet been sabotaged by our culture's obsession with stimulation and thrill-seeking. Unfortunately, all too soon, we help them get caught up in the world of watching too many movies, fast-moving learning tools—toys that talk, make noises, play music, swirl and twirl. All too soon we hear these words, "I'm bored; there's nothing to do."

Pleasure Is in the Waiting

I tell my family members that I don't like surprises. Please tell me what you are planning so that I can enjoy the delicious anticipation of what is to come. I always explain that the best part for me is the waiting for an event, a gift or a trip.

I can clearly remember when I was eleven years old and fantasized about having my very own pair of figure skates. I lived in Prince George, British Columbia, Canada at the time, and the popular outdoor activity in the winter was ice skating. I would lie awake at night and dream about wearing those gorgeous white skates and twirling effortlessly in figure eights on the ice. I begged for skates to be under the Christmas tree that year, and for the longest time it was all I could think about. The tradition in our home was to open presents on Christmas Eve, and finally after finishing our celebrations at our church, it was time to explore the treasures under the tree. There was one mysterious box under the tree that held my magical, beautiful, coveted skates. For years I slung those skates over my shoulder to join my friends on the ice, and each time I laced up those long white laces, I felt a sense of pride at owning those beautiful figure skates. Those skates still hang on a nail in my basement and even as I write this, I can still remember the thrill of opening that box on Christmas Eve.

My husband Jack tells a different story. For Christmas one year he coveted a table hockey game and he wanted it so badly that he went searching through the whole house to see if he could find it. He did find it under a bed, but when Christmas morning arrived the thrill of this present was gone because he had not waited.

We think that we will be happiest when we get what we want when we want it. But Dr. Dehart goes on to say, "You may think that getting what we want should build pleasure—after all, our pleasure comes instantly. But the problem with instant gratification is it bypasses normal pleasure-inducing mechanisms, like the joy of anticipating the gift your father has promised for your birthday. The pleasure is in the waiting, in anticipating something very special that is yet to happen, not the actual receiving. When it comes instantly, the pleasure passes away just as quickly."[49]

The very things we think will make us happiest in the moment actually have the prospect to rob us of future joy.

Making Space for God's Pleasure

We are spiritual beings and nothing in this material world will completely quench our thirst for satisfaction. Unfortunately, even our churches have gotten on board with the constant stimulation of videos, flashing screens, lights and dancing girls. We need our churches to help us with our spiritual formation so that we have the power to navigate through this noisy, flashy clutter and live the joyful, abundant life that Jesus said was available to us.

We need to be reminded that there is a supernatural power available to us that will fill us with lasting pleasure called joy. When we tap into God's resources, we will find the kind of fulfillment that will leave us satisfied. Unfortunately, in order to find this resource, we have to stop, wait and listen. We don't make time these days to be silent, unstimulated and focused on knowing God. But the Bible tells us that this is the way to know our God; "Be still, and know that I am God" (Psalm 46:10, NIV).

Our pace of life has accelerated, and most people I know hate waiting. We don't want anything to slow us down:

- Got a headache or any kind of pain in your body? There is a pill for everything.
- Need some money? Transfer it into your bank account online.
- Need to talk to someone? E-mail or text them.
- If you are an author and a speaker, you can reach your audience by blogging, Facebooking, Twittering, doing a trailer, Godtubing, and podcasting.
- Need some information? Google.

We are an instant culture, and I am afraid we have forgotten that we need to make space in our lives for God to nurture our soul, to find our purpose and to discover our pleasure in Him. We need to be intentional about returning to some spiritual disciplines and to places of isolation away from the noise of the world so that in this silence we can hear the whispers of God. This is the place where we learn to live and walk according to God's desires for us, a place where we listen to what the Spirit of God needs to say to us about walking in the Spirit.

"Those who live according to the sinful nature have their minds set on what that nature desires; but those who live in accordance with the Spirit have their minds set on what the Spirit desires. The mind of sinful man is death, but the mind controlled by the Spirit is life and peace" (Rom. 8:5-6, NIV).

To live in accordance with the Spirit, we need to be in relationship with the Spirit of God. It is of utmost importance to spend quality, intentional time to make any relationship work, and that applies to our relationship with God, the One who created us, who knows us intimately and is the One who will bring us lasting pleasure. You are the one who needs to decide what your relationship with God will look like in your life.

In the Psalms, David said it in such a beautiful way: "In the morning, O Lord, you hear my voice; in the morning I lay my requests before you and wait in expectation" (Psalm 5:3, NIV).

I am like David; I love to spend time with God in the morning. I curl up in my wing chair to watch the sun come up over the mountains, and see the morning light awaken the sky to paint it with its gorgeous colors. Day after day I am reminded of the beauty of God as I watch the seasons unfold before me. I see leaves bursting out of their branches in the spring, and in the winter snowflakes cover the evergreens like the sprinkling of icing sugar. As I behold His creation, and discover His beautiful promises for me in the Bible, my mind is set on God, and that lays the foundation for my day. My time with Him awakens my soul to what the Spirit of God wants to do through me that day. It makes me attentive to what is going on around me so that I can intentionally love and be alert to ways I can help or bless people.

When I am in tune with the Spirit, I am more aware when my attitude is lousy—when I feel unfulfilled and yearn to reach for pleasure that I know will harm me. When I intentionally tap into the Spirit of God I am given the power to overcome offenses and jealousy. If I don't spend time with

God, my mind will be numb to His whispers that help me find my way through days that go at warp speed or have the potential to corrupt my mind and frustrate me horribly.

Over the last year I have been praying this prayer almost every morning: "God, help me to do today what I need to do today, no more, no less; to bring glory to Your name." Through this simple prayer God has faithfully and almost effortlessly scheduled my days and weeks so that everything that needs to be done gets done.

Expectant Waiting

Frankly, I also do not like waiting. I see it as a weapon of mass distraction ruining my precious time. I'm like the little child in the back seat of the car impatiently pleading and whining, "Are we there yet? When are we going to get there?"

God has been teaching me a different kind of waiting because life seems stormy these days. Gas prices are soaring out of sight, there are too many divorces, house prices are outrageously high, friends are battling with fatigue and depression, my mother's health is failing and a hurricane has struck again. We are bombarded with too much information and have too little time. Lately I seem to be standing in the middle of storms where I feel shaken and know I need to hang onto something strong so that I won't be swept away. Then I remember hearing a story about the chicken and the eagle.

When a storm comes, chickens run around madly flapping their wings, squawking, going in circles, digging in the same old dirt and going nowhere. The eagle is different. When it sees a storm coming, it sits on a rock and waits. When the storm comes it rises up to "catch the wind" so that it will take the eagle to higher heights—soaring on the strength of the wind. In fact, the eagle uses the storms to lift it higher than it would normally go.

When I have the least energy or desire to pray, this is exactly the time I need to do it. I need to stop and rest on the rock, Jesus Christ, and ask Him to open new doors of opportunity, heal my heart, give me new energy, and change my perspective. Then I need to *wait expectantly* because I know from past experiences that God has used all my disappointments, grief and failures to make me more resilient and beautiful, from the inside out.

- Through my husband's death, He taught me what is important and what useless stuff is.
- Through lost speaking opportunities, He gave me ever better ones.
- Through trusting Him with my finances, He has proven to me that He always provides.
- Through the storm of waiting for other people to change, He taught me that I had to change.

Expectant waiting is not aimlessly sitting in the front of the TV in yesterday's pajamas, flicking channels, munching on junk food and blindly wishing that the next day will be different; it is giving our fears, doubts and longings to God and knowing that He will stop the storm and burst forth new beauty in His time.

My daughter Michelle experienced expectant waiting and she tells it this way:

> When I think back on fourteen years of infertility, one thing that stands out in my mind is the waiting. My husband Tim and I waited for test results, waited to see if treatments would work, and each month we anxiously waited for some kind of result. When we decided to adopt, we had to wait to be matched with a birth mother, wait for the phone call that the baby was born and wait to see if the baby would be ours. The waiting seemed endless. The incredible longing in my heart for a baby was so very painful at times. The only thought that got me through this endless waiting was the belief that there was a purpose to it all. As a Christian, I believe that God loves me and that His plans are greater than mine, and that He won't let me suffer forever.

There were definitely times when I questioned this. Our second attempt to adopt a baby ended in a painful, unsuccessful end. I could not see any light at the end of the tunnel. Two close friends gave me the same verse, "Yet God has made everything beautiful for its own time" (Eccl. 3:11, NLT). Around this time God kept bringing my thoughts and attention to butterflies. The verse and the butterflies seemed to go together so well, and I knew that God was showing me, in His kind way, that something beautiful would emerge from this pain. This gave me the courage to give my desires and pain over to God. We had decided not to try to adopt again, but God was in the background with other plans. After more waiting, we finally had another baby boy, and I felt that God had been so faithful in giving us the desire of our hearts.

This was a season of incredible contentment, but there was still a silent yearning in my heart for a little girl. God then gave us a miracle; I became pregnant and it was a girl. It came at a time when I hadn't been waiting for it, but in His time. Sometimes our expectant waiting can turn out unexpectedly.

Through the waiting, I learned that I don't know how the story will end, but I learned what it really means to trust God. I can truly say that God made everything beautiful in His time. He did more for me than I could have ever imagined. I continue to put my trust in Him daily as I raise my family.

Soaring Like an Eagle

We are exhausted and frustrated people these days. When we plow through our days in a state of fatigue, we desperately reach for the quickest, easiest and most accessible pleasure that will bring instant relief. It's almost as if our brain is saying, "I need something to make me feel better, and I need it now!"

In a *Purpose-Driven Life* devotional, Rick Warren gave these statistics: "A lot of people are on overload and headed for a crash…. People now sleep 2 1/2 fewer hours each night than people did a hundred years ago. The average work week is longer now than it was in the 1960s. The average office worker has 36 hours of work piled up on his or her desk. It takes us three hours a week just to sort through it and find what we need. We spend eight months of our lives opening junk mail, two years of our lives playing phone tag with people, and five years waiting for people who are late for meetings."[50]

I believe we discover our greatest delight in life when we are not weary and when we are wide awake enough to see and appreciate the simple pleasures right before our eyes. However, it entails doing something that goes against our natural instinct, and that is to slow down, get more rest, and *wait expectantly for God to schedule our hours and our days.*

How amazing it would be if we gave ourselves permission to get more sleep and to take the time to enjoy the simple pleasures that have been given us to:

- Have regular meal times with our families, talking about our hopes, goals, and disappointments.
- Walk with a friend and share funny stories.
- Stand in line at a grocery store and take the time to ask the cashier what she will do when she goes home.
- Not check our text messages or e-mails for three days.
- Bake a chocolate cake.
- Light fifty candles and play our favorite music.
- Sit in the tub and read a favorite new novel.
- Paint our toenails a different color.
- Buy ourselves fresh flowers and place them in several vases around the house.
- Go for a walk and ask God to show us a delicious delight.

When we slow down and allow God to arrange our days, He will renew our strength and show us His pleasures that will fill and satisfy us.

"But those who trust in the Lord will find new strength. They will soar high on wings like eagles. They will run and not grow weary. They will walk and not faint" (Isa. 40:31, NLT).

What an amazing experience it must be to soar like an eagle, high above the clouds, effortlessly floating along on wind that was placed there for your pleasure. I believe this is a possibility for all of us if we *choose* to wait expectantly for God to unfold His plans and purposes for each of our days.

Dr. Hart explains that we need to learn and choose to become satisfied. "There is no limit to the craving for pleasure. This pleasure is a barrel without a bottom—it never gets full. The more you give it, the more it wants....[51] Despite having more sources of pleasure than ever before in history, we are probably the unhappiest people who have ever lived."[52]

You and God are the only ones who have the power to choose the kind of pleasures that will give you a full and satisfying life. To do this you need to present your heart's desires, concerns and requests to God and then let him unfold them in his perfect timing. God is as close as your next breath and prayer.

"The Lord is fair in everything he does, and full of kindness. He is close to all who call on him sincerely. He fulfills the desires of those who reverence and trust him; he hears their cries for help and rescues them" (Psalm 145:17-19, TLB).

When we manipulate people and circumstances in our life to get what we think we want or need, it is rarely ours to keep. Only God can give us what we really need. He is the only one who knows because He is the one who created us. Many of us bring misery upon ourselves with our choices for instant gratification. Choose to wait and check out the long-term ramifications of your choices:

Choices That Enrich Your Life

1. That man at work is evoking feelings you haven't experienced in a long time. He is making you feel beautiful, smart, and treats you

better than your husband. Stop and choose to wait and identify those feelings. Think ahead to the ramifications of what this will do to your marriage, your family—your soul.

2. A new job opportunity opens up with a better salary. Choose to wait and check out all the pros and cons of both jobs. Money is not always the answer for satisfaction at your workplace.

3. You heard that a friend said something hurtful about you behind your back. Before you give in to the pleasure of blasting angry words at her, choose to wait and find out the truth.

4. You just saw a sign that said you could buy a new vehicle with zero dollars down and payments that won't start for three months. Choose to wait and see if you really do need a new vehicle and if these payments will fit into your already stretched monthly budget.

5. You've had a lousy day at work, you've been sitting in traffic too much, you're tired and you deserve some gratification. You're going to stop at a lounge and have a few drinks before you go home. Wait and think about the fact that you will be drinking and driving.

6. You finally get a marriage proposal. Ask yourself, "Is this the man that I want to spend the rest of my life with?" Wait expectantly for God's whispers to affirm that this man has the values and character of a good husband for you.

7. You secretly find pleasure in surfing the internet for pornographic images. Stop and think about how this will affect your spouse and children when they discover this little secret. Give your desires to God and wait for Him to fill them with something that will give you satisfaction and not guilt.

8. Gambling has been fun so far. Choose to stop it before it affects your finances and other areas of your life.

9. Your heart's desire has been to have a house full of children but you find that you are infertile. Wait expectantly with God to help you determine which avenue you should take to help you fill your home with children.

10. You feel unappreciated, lonely and tired. Before you go to the fridge again for more food, stop and choose to think about what this is doing to your body.

11. Your son or daughter is not living a life that is honoring God. Choose to pray and wait expectantly for God to work out His plans and purposes in your children's lives. Choose to do this daily, even if it takes the rest of your life.

12. You have written a manuscript, a song or poem and nobody will publish it for you. Give your passions and requests to God and He will open the door at the right time and place.

Stop and Ask God To Help You Change Sand to Pearls

Begin by asking: God, am I seeking the right pleasures?

S Scripture: "The Lord is fair in everything he does, and full of kindness. He is close to all who call on him sincerely. He fulfills the desires of those who reverence and trust him; he hears their cries for help and rescues them" (Psalm 145:17-19, TLB).

T Thanksgiving: God, in this world with its many expectations, I need someone to be fair and kind to me. Thank You, God, for Your gentleness in reminding me that You hear my cry for help and that You will rescue me from the demands of the world, and from myself. Thank You that You will fulfill me with the kind of desires that will bring me satisfaction and not destruction.

O Observation: God, the world seems harsh and demanding these days, and when I read this promise that You will rescue me, I am overwhelmed with gratitude and relief. God, I do cry to You and ask You to help me find the kind of pleasures that will fill me so that I don't get tempted with those things that have the potential to harm me.

P Prayer: The world is throwing so many temptations at me these days that I need divine insight into what is good for me, and what has the capability to send me down the wrong path.

Sometimes, God, I want things so badly that I don't even realize I am manipulating people and events to get what I want. Teach me and help me to wait when I need to wait for You to unfold Your plans and purposes for my life. The kind of purposes that will give me the ultimate pleasures of knowing I am in Your will and part of Your Kingdom work here on earth. Show me how to be still, to get enough sleep and to listen for the whispers of Your voice telling me where to go, what to do and when to wait expectantly for You. During my days of making hundreds of choices, I ask You to walk alongside me and help me make the kind of choices that will ultimately fulfill the desires of my heart. Thank You.

Amen.

Chapter 8

Comparing or Contentment

An Ugly, Slow Burn

Cheerfulness and contentment are great beautifiers
and are famous preservers of youthful looks.

—CHARLES DICKENS

What you have looks better than what I have" begins the slow, ugly burn of jealousy. When I was seven, I wanted black shiny shoes and a fold-out pencil box just like the other girls in my glass. As a teenager I compared lipstick colors, stretch pants, haircuts, reversible skirts and matching sweaters. In my mind I thought, *If I could have_____, it would feel like I had arrived and was part of the popular crowd.* Even when I did have a boyfriend, he was not as popular as my friend Carleen's boyfriend, who had curly hair and drove his very own sleek red and white Pontiac.

There is no end of comparing, wanting or keeping up. Just look at fashion: one day you feel like a queen because you are wearing the latest bell-bottom pants. The next year, its back to skinny pants, and your pants look dumb. How can a woman feel contentment when the rules and standards always change?

Me, Jealous?

That's right, I have no trouble with wanting the kind of house, donkey or oxen that my neighbor has. "You shall not covet your neighbor's house. You shall not covet your neighbor's wife, or his manservant or maidservant, his ox or donkey, or anything that belongs to your neighbor" (Exod. 20:17, NIV). None of this is troublesome for me. Not only that, I can confidently say that I am not jealous of my friends who have tons of money, three houses, a yacht, and endless cash flow. I am thrilled for people who have a successful career, a great golf score or own all the gorgeous furniture and clothes they want.

A few years ago, I bragged to my friend Joanne that I was now immune to the fangs of the green, ugly monster of jealousy. She seemed amused and asked me a simple, profound question, "Do you think those feelings ever leave us?" Those words reverberated in my ears that night as I sat in a circle with a group of women who were sharing stories of what God was doing in their lives. I celebrated, and cried with joy for them until someone shared something God was doing in her life. *That's exactly what I want! How come she got to have it and not me?* I struggled to fight off the familiar feelings creeping up my spine—a slow, ugly burn.

As I walked out the door with Joanne that night, we laughed and chatted about our evening. Something in my voice made her look into my eyes, and she said, "Heidi, something happened in there to make you jealous, didn't it?" Caught, with no way of escape! I agreed with her and we laughed about it, but that menacing fiend jealousy taunted me all the way home. I had to examine my feelings. An opportunity I was incredibly passionate about had been given to someone else. I felt hurt, devalued and overlooked. *What about me? When is it finally my turn?*

When I compare myself to others, I am in fact saying to God that I don't believe I trust Him with my life. He is blessing someone else more than me. Long after that night, I thought, *What is wrong with me? Why am I being overlooked? Am I not good enough or smart enough? Have I not done enough Kingdom work here on earth to balance off a little reward now and then? When I compare myself to that woman in the circle, I think I have worked harder. So why is she the one getting what I really want?*

A mammoth jealousy like this, left unattended, can make us crazy and chase away any hope of contentment. It is a slow burn that consumes our thoughts, puts poison on our tongues, clouds our reasoning and plots revenge. Cheryl, a beautiful young woman that I have known for many years expresses her struggle this way:

> Many of us have heard the saying "Anything you can do, I can do better." Many of us spend much of our time wishing we had what the "Joneses" had. We want the latest gizmo, the big house, new car or that trend-setting fashion piece we can't live without.
>
> A huge struggle for me in high school was not being happy with what I had. My friend Janelle seemed to have it all: a loving family with two parents, an older sister and two younger brothers, and an adorable dog. She always lived in beautiful homes, had trendy clothes; and to top it off, she was gorgeous. There I was; I only had a single mom, one younger sister and we rented a low-income housing unit. My home was broken, and through my eyes, Janelle's was perfect. Janelle even seemed to be the perfect Christian, whereas I felt like I was always failing and felt that surely God had given up on me. Janelle and I were good friends in high school but I often found it hard to love her because I was constantly comparing myself to her. My frustrations with my lot in life led to bitterness and resentment on my part and it nearly destroyed our friendship.
>
> As we left high school and moved forward in life, God began to teach me that He made me unique and all the imperfections in my life were just the way He wanted it. He would use my circumstances for His glory. I began to see the beauty in my life, and I was able to see myself as physically beautiful. I truly gained confidence; but it was

a God confidence. As my relationship with my Creator grew, I began to see Janelle through His eyes. She still had all the things from before; however, instead of resenting them, I began to appreciate them.

Interestingly enough, people only seem perfect because of how we view them. I had a narrow view of her life because I didn't know some of the struggles Janelle had. I think if we took a second look at the "Joneses" we so admire, we would see that they also have struggles. We also need to stop and thank God for the things we do have because He has provided so richly for us. Today, Janelle and I are great friends. We have seen each other through much and I am confident that we will be lifelong friends. [53]

Lethal Emotions, Deadly Endings

We have been struggling with this lethal emotion since the beginning of time—it always ends up badly: favoritism in families causes division.

a. Lethal Emotions—Joseph, the beloved son of Israel, had been given a gorgeous, multicolored coat that flaunted favoritism. His brothers had to listen to him brag about how they would all have to bow down to him, and how he would reign over them. People don't enjoy having superiority shoved down their throats. The Bible said, "His brothers were jealous of him" (Genesis 37:11, NIV). It was visibly obvious that their father loved Joseph more than them, and they were sick and tired of playing second fiddle to a young, boastful, immature braggart. "'Here comes that dreamer!' they said to each other. 'Come now, let's kill him and throw him into one of these cisterns and say that a ferocious animal devoured him. Then we'll see what comes of his dreams'" (Genesis 37:19-20, NIV).

This unbridled jealousy burst into rage that caused Joseph's brothers to plot a murder, lie, sell their brother into slavery, cover up a murder, and watch their father mourn for his beloved son for the next eleven years.

b. Deadly Endings—Beware when someone else gets the credit. A simple slingshot and five smooth stones were the beginning of a love-hate relationship that had the making of an epic movie. King Saul's appreciation for a harp-playing shepherd boy turned into revengeful rivalry when he heard: *"Saul has slain his thousands, and David his tens of thousands."*

This refrain galled Saul. "'They have credited David with tens of thousands,' he thought, 'but me with only thousands. What more can he get but the kingdom?' And from that time on Saul kept a jealous eye on David" (1 Sam. 18:6-9, NIV). Once jealousy gripped King Saul, it drove him into a frenzy of revenge, and ultimately made him go mad and kill himself.

When we have been given a special leadership position, moved ahead in a company, have been appointed to do a special ministry or perhaps finally finished a tough task, we feel we deserve honor and credit. The green fuel starts to burn when that credit is given to someone else. Jealousy colors our thinking and propels us into irrational behavior that has the ability to destroy relationships, ministries, marriages and families. Everything.

Who's on First?

Even though we won't often admit it, we want to be first, number one, the best. It was so much easier when we went to school; we brought home a report card that told us if we were smart and socially acceptable. Now the only way to measure how we are doing is by looking around and checking the competition:

- The size of our houses and the cars in our driveway.
- The labels on our clothes.
- How many activities our children are involved in.
- Who has the best bike, boat, golf clubs or vacation.
- How many people attend our Sunday morning services.
- Who got a raise besides us.

It all ends in "how many" and "how much."

Rick Warren in his book, *The Purpose-Driven Life*, devotes an entire chapter to discovering our purpose in life so that we don't compare ourselves to anyone else. He says, "Satan will try to steal the joy of service from you in a couple of ways: by tempting you to *compare* your ministry with others, and by tempting you to *conform* your ministry to the expectations of others. Both are deadly traps that will distract you from serving in the ways God intended." [54]

Learning To Be Content

Many of us hope that as we get older, jealousy will just go away one day, and one day contentment will show up at our front door. It doesn't.

The apostle Paul was a man blessed with every privilege. He had the best of everything: education, position, noble genealogy, reputation. But when he gave his life over to God, he was beaten, put in prison, starved, shipwrecked and stripped of his clothes and everything he had.

What in the world would compel someone to follow God's pathway and experience this kind of injustice, discomfort and pain? Here is what Paul says: "I know what it is to be in need, and I know what it is to have plenty. I have learned the secret of being content in any and every situation, whether well fed or hungry, whether living in plenty or in want. I can do everything through him who gives me strength" (Phil. 4:12-13, NIV).

He says, "He has *learned* the secret." To learn this secret ourselves, we have to stop and re-evaluate our thinking. We can achieve this with these five careful steps.

1. Find Our Where Your Feelings Come From

We do not need to succumb to letting feelings determining our choices. Women are gorgeous creatures loaded with emotions. We need to discover that we can make better choices by learning to identify the thoughts that cause our negative feelings. Here is what Dallas Willard says in his book *Renovation of the Heart*: "So if we are formed in Christ's likeness, we must take good care of our feelings and not just let them happen." [55]

Our feelings come from our thoughts, so in order to change our feelings, we need to change our thoughts. Yes, we can do this! First, we must identify which words we heard or read that caused us to think a particular thought.

- If I *heard* that someone got something I wanted, this may cause me to be jealous.
- If I *read* an e-mail, letter or book that suggested I was being over-looked, that I missed out on something, or lacked something I wanted, those words may provoke a slow, ugly burn.

Now that we have the *words* which created our thoughts, we have the power to change our feelings.

2. Change The Words

We need to remind ourselves that God made each one of us unique, and we are each like nobody else. Change the words. Instead of ruminating on the words that led to a particular hurtful or unpleasant thought, put these words in your heart and spirit: God is perfect, and He has a perfect choice for each of us that is unlike what He has chosen for anyone else.

"Make a careful exploration of who you are and the work you have been given, and then sink yourself into that. Don't be impressed with yourself. Don't compare yourself with others. Each of you must take responsibility for doing the creative best you can with your own life" (Gal. 6:4, MSG).

These are powerful, truthful words, and they need to be the plumb line of truth when our eyes start focusing on what belongs to others.

When I sense the recognizable, prickly emotions of jealousy rising up in me, here is what I need to do:

- Stop, search my heart and recall the words that caused my feelings.
- Admit the truth that jealousy is ugly, and it is a sin. "But if you harbor bitter envy and selfish ambition in your hearts, do not boast about it or deny the truth" (James 3:14, NIV).
- Examine my area of insecurity, and unpack the lies that are going through my head.
- Intentionally focus on God's words of truth for me in that particular situation. I need to focus on the fact that I am a work in

progress. "Being confident of this, that he who began a good work in you will carry it on to completion until the day of Christ Jesus" (Phil. 1:6, NIV).

- Remind myself that God's plan for my life has been uniquely designed only for me.
- Then, I need to do the next step: be grateful.

3. Say "Danke Shoen"

When I was a little girl living in Germany, I was taught to say *danke shoen*—thank you. It wasn't something that came naturally for me as a young child; my parents had to teach me the art of being grateful for gifts and other people's generous efforts. Being grateful is not instinctive; humanly speaking we are all very selfish. Gratefulness, along with contentment, has to be learned.

I have to stop and remind myself of the good things in my life, especially the ones I take for granted. I thank God for my hot showers in the morning, a car in my driveway, a great pair of jeans, my new laptop, lunch with a friend, a new book sitting on my bedside table. I am so grateful for my husband, children, grandchildren and friends. These are all tangible evidence of God's goodness poured out on me.

When I stop and say the words, "Thank you," they stop the feeling of "life is not fair; I am being overlooked." They make me refocus on the person to whom I am giving thanks, Jesus, who knows what is the very best for me in everything.

"I thank Christ Jesus our Lord, who has given me strength, that he considered me faithful, appointing me to his service" (1 Tim. 1:12, NIV). In this verse the word "thank" in the Greek is *charis*, "the divine influence upon the heart, and its reflection in the life; (including gratitude): acceptable benefit, favor, gift, grace (-ious), joy liberality, pleasure."[56]

With each utterance of "thank you," God gives us the strength to reflect on all the gifts He has given us. Soon envy disappears into a foggy distance. Contentment shows up.

4. Crank Up a Celebration

I discovered this unique way of overcoming jealousy by listening to Andy Stanley, on his 2007 series *The Best of Catalyst*.[57] I have noticed how it is much easier to mourn with those who mourn than rejoice with those who rejoice. But it is precisely when we rejoice with others that we destroy the toxic comparison trap.

I am finally maturing enough to understand that God knows better than I do what I can handle. I can relax knowing there are enough opportunities out there for everyone, and if I am given too much too soon, I will crumble under the added pressure. Transformation begins in my heart when God gives me the grace to pour blessings onto other people's lives—when I say to someone, "I bless you in your new ministry. I bless you for the new project you are taking on. I bless you for leading that great Bible Study. I bless you for taking that initiative. I bless you as you do that interview on the platform today. I bless you as you write your new book." In these strategic moments He pours freedom and blessings back on me. Then I can honestly rejoice with others.

In the Garden of Eden, Eve took her eyes off God and started looking at the tree. Each time we take our eyes off God and look at something that doesn't belong to us, it causes us pain and trouble.

5. Consider Whether To Tell or Not To Tell

I have women ask me, "When I am struggling with jealousy, should I tell that person?"

There are two camps:

    a. Tell the person you are jealous of them.

        I believe this should be done only under careful and prayerful consideration. If it is not communicated carefully, it will destroy the relationship rather than mend it. Jealousy never completely evaporates, so the other person will continue to wonder, "When will I make that person jealous again?"

b. Jealousy is our own issue.

Unless the other person is deliberately evoking jealousy in you, work it out in your own heart with God. Jealousy reveals a lack of confidence in your own life. You cannot expect other people to adjust their lives and conversations to meet and heal your insecurities.

In this competitive world, I find that being content is one of the most gorgeous gifts God has given me. I long for that day when, no matter how fast and hard the world whirls around me, I can say, "I have learned to be content in all circumstances."

Let's be frank: jealousy will not go away overnight. We are on a pathway where God continually shapes us into the people He designed us to be. Let's change the words "I want what you have" to "I want what God has for me."

Choices That Enrich Your Life

1. When someone else gets a raise, choose to celebrate that person. Also ask yourself, "Is there a reason I am not getting a raise? Are there areas I need to improve?"

2. Your best friend is getting married, and you're not. Diligently pray and choose to believe that God is your husband and provider until such time as the right man comes along for you.

3. You didn't get invited to an event that was very important to you. Choose to let it go, and wait for another opportunity.

4. An outfit you have been eyeing in the store is now being worn by your friend. Choose to compliment her on it and let her enjoy it. Your time will come.

5. Other women are getting more work opportunities than you. Choose to believe that God's timing is always perfect, and that He knows exactly what you can handle.

6. Someone just got recognized for something you created. You have

been overlooked! Don't overreact. Choose to believe there are other opportunities waiting for you to excel in.

7. Your rival just accomplished something you have been working for. Choose to believe that the other person is not a "thing" but one of God's creatures that has also been given unique gifts and opportunities in this Kingdom here on earth.

8. Someone you admire has a "Martha Stewart" home, and it leaves you green with envy every time you go there. Choose to enjoy her hospitality and beautiful surroundings. Perhaps you can learn something from her. Choose to ask her—she might be thrilled to help you.

9. Everyone seems so happy, and your life feels like one big mess. Choose to believe that the only happiness we find is by trusting God to guide our lives. Today ask God to help you make a fresh start.

10. You have a problem with rich people. Choose to acknowledge your jealousy, and count the blessings in your own life. Remember when we leave this world we can't take anything with us.

Stop and Ask God To Help You Change Sand to Pearls

Begin by asking: "What makes me feel overlooked?"

S Scripture: "I know what it is to be in need, and I know what it is to have plenty. I have learned the secret of being content in any and every situation, whether well fed or hungry, whether living in plenty or in want. I can do everything through him who gives me strength" (Phil. 4:12-13, NIV).

T Thanksgiving: Thank You, God, that You will reveal Your secrets to me about how I can be content. I know that You have made me unique, and that Your plan for my life is like no one else's. Thank You that You will reveal Yourself to me in ways that I can comprehend. Thank You for being so kind with me when I stumble and fall.

O Observation: God, I realize it is my responsibility to move from envy to contentment, but I can't travel this road alone. I desperately need You when the ugly burn begins in my heart. I believe that You will continue to faithfully shape me into the woman You created me to be. Help me to trust You every step of the way.

P Prayer: God, I confess that I am an insecure human being with need for constant affirmation of who I am. I recognize that I look around at other people's lives and accomplishments to measure how I am doing. Forgive me when I take my eyes off You and the abundance of blessings You have so graciously placed in my life. Forgive me when I think someone else has been blessed more than me, and that I have been overlooked. I know that You never overlook me—that You know every hair on my head, every desire in my heart, and every thought in my mind. Help me to run to the truth of Your written word to find solace, comfort and reassurance when I feel the pain of insecurity rising up in me. I long for contentment: teach me every day to seek You so that I find that contentment in knowing You more intimately. Help me to check my words when I feel the ugly, slow burn of jealousy searing my soul. I pray that one day these feelings will be unrecognizable in my life, and that the Son of God will make it disappear like a morning mist. Thank You that You continue to teach me, and that You never give up on me.

Amen.

Chapter 9

Fear or Fortitude

This World Is Not a Safe Place

Fear defeats more people than any other one thing in the world.

—RALPH WALDO EMERSON

I could not cave in and say "no" to this challenging invitation. My grandson Ryan's eyes pleaded with me to say "yes" to a biking adventure on the Myra Canyon trestles. It was an exciting yet daunting request. It was exciting because the Myra Canyon trestles finally reopened on June 22, 2008, after the closing because of destruction of the 2003 Firestorm fire, and daunting because I had not been on a bike for a number of years. Worse yet was that I was afraid of heights—especially train trestles.

My first glimpse of the trestles took my breath away. The ongoing restoration of the trestles has fascinated me, but I had no idea they were so high, beautiful and narrow and that there were so many of them. I could see that once we went over all eighteen of them for twelve kilometers, we would have to come back the same way. That meant thirty-six trestles and twenty-four kilometers of biking trail. This was more than I had bargained for but there was no way out. I had to live up to my reputation of being the "adventurous Nana," one who was up to any challenge, or ready for any competition.

We started with the backward route: trestle No. 18. I watched as my grandson Ryan and his mom Janice gracefully rode across it. I chose a safer route—a small side trail. Approaching the intimidating, narrow Trestle No. 17 compelled me to get off my bike and walk across. Janice saw me walking and gently shouted, "Hey Mom, there are thirty-four more trestles; are you going to walk across all of them?"

Inwardly I winced and shrank back from those provoking words; however I knew that decision time had come. It was time to hike up my princess socks and pull fortitude out of my back pocket.

Fortitude means strength, courage, guts, staying power, grit, determination, endurance and resilience. I honestly believed I had all of those; but somewhere in the past fear had entered into the equation. Over the last two decades I uncovered the horrible realization that if we surrender to it, fear has the power to diminish and override every aspect of fortitude.

Trap Door Opens

In my thirties I sadly discovered that this world was no longer safe. On a clear, blue sky day of October 27, 1985, in Lethbridge, Alberta, two fathers took three of their children for a leisurely Sunday excursion down a river that runs around the city of Lethbridge. In the midst of this colorful, majestic and calm excursion down the Old Man River, their dingy encountered a treacherous eddy. An eddy is a swirling pool of water that is in variance with the main current of water, and it is so powerful it has the ability to take a boat, dingy or raft and suck it into its vortex. That is exactly what happened. Ryan Imbach, age seven, Jamie Derksen, age ten, and his sister Marina Joy Derksen, age seven, all drowned. In that exact time frame, another friend of mine called me and asked me to hurry and meet her in the hospital in Lethbridge, Alberta. Her eight-year-old son had been struck by a vehicle and was seriously injured. He died before I arrived at the hospital. In the following week I went to two funerals, saw four little white coffins, and watched my friends suffer the excruciating pain of losing the most precious gifts in their life—their children.

It was almost as if my mind had allowed a trap door to be opened, and it revealed monsters I had never seen before. I became fearful.

- I was afraid someone I loved would die.
- I feared heights.
- As my children got older and started to drive, I feared for their lives every time they got into their cars.
- I feared I would never find my purpose in life.
- I feared I would never be loveable enough.

As the years went on I hated fear, but it continued to follow me around, to intimidate and haunt me. Schools no longer were safe places for my children when I heard that Eric Harris and Dylan Klebold entered Columbine High School on April 20, 1999, and killed thirteen of their classmates and teachers. That was four years after Timothy McVeigh killed 168 fellow citizens in Oklahoma City with a truck bomb outside the Alfred P. Murrah Federal Building. We all watched in horror and disbelief as planes flew through the World Trade Center on September 11, 2001, destroying a beautiful, defining landmark and killing thousands of humans. The words tsunami, terrorism, fraud, hurricanes, earthquakes and suicide bombers have become part of familiar household conversations; but still my heart pounds a little harder and is a little sadder each time I hear of them on a newscast. I never signed a consent form saying that fear had permission to enter my life, but once the fear trap door was opened, very little felt safe.

One of the most pervasive and crippling emotions is fear. It stops us from experiencing who we are, who God is, and why we have been placed here on earth. The dictionary defines fear as "a distressing emotion aroused by an impending pain, danger, evil, etc., or by the illusion of such."[58]

Fear Robs Us of Our Power

It is the word "illusion" that can create its own script of a negative future that can make us feel defenseless. If we really think about it, we are rehearsing a negative future and allowing something that has not yet happened to rob us and drain us of energy, creativity and joy.

I sometimes ask women at a workshop or retreat, "What are you afraid of?" From hearing their answers, I conclude that we all have been afraid of something from the time we were born.

Through:

- Listening to adults talk about fearful things.
- Feeling stupid when we fail in sports, spelling bees and tests.
- Imagining spiders, snakes and monsters under our beds.
- Hearing, "Don't touch that, it's hot." "Careful, you'll hurt yourself." "Don't take any rides with strangers." "You'll never win if you play like that."
- Watching marriages break up, houses burning and feeling bones break.
- Watching scary movies.

It seems bizarre but we continue to feed each other with fear. Just this week I attended a baby shower, and of course when we are at this type of event the room is full of women talking about babies. I sat back and listened to the chatter alerting my pregnant friend about the upcoming sleepless nights, horrors of breastfeeding, placing the baby properly so it won't die in its sleep, the safety of baby equipment so that the baby won't get strangled, the proper car seat, diapers—the list of cautions and possible dangers was endless. I watched my pregnant friend's eyes get bigger and bigger with fear. Is there an unconscious pleasure in projecting our fears so that we know we are not suffering alone?

There are three different kinds of fear:

1. Reverential Fear

The first one is acknowledging the presence and power of a Holy God whose thoughts are never far from us. We must never forget that He is the great I Am, the Omega, Elohiym, Yehovah. Knowing this amazing, powerful God is the beginning of wisdom and it gives us power to obey Him and stop sinning. This is the wisdom we need to give us insight into knowing the difference between a destructive and diminishing fear and a beneficial fear that motivates us to make a good choice. "How does a man become wise? The first step is to trust and reverence the Lord" (Prov. 1:7, TLB).

2. Self-Preserving Fear

This is the positive side of fear, an emotion which enables us to sense danger. It is to help us avert accidents or protect ourselves or those we love. This fear motivated our parents to tell us to "look both ways before you cross the street" and it compels us to see a doctor when we feel a lump in a breast or sense a "red flag" in our relationships. If we understand that it is a helpful emotion, we can give it permission to give us energy and humility to do our best in difficult and stressful situations.

3. Slavish Fear

The Greek noun for fear is *delia*, "that spirit is not given us of God. The word denotes cowardice and timidity and is never used in a good sense."[59] This is a destructive fear and renders us powerless. It cripples our emotions and stops us from fulfilling our God-given potential while we are on earth.

Fear becomes irrational when it controls and interferes with our relationships, daily activities and following after our life's purpose. Fear can become so intense that it can come packaged with a racing heart, breathing difficulty, cold sweats and feeling as though our knees will crumble under us. It can be completely unreasonable and cause incredible suffering. Intense fear that is focused on a particular situation or object can be described as a phobia, and there are 530 documented phobias.[60] Avoiding the reality of these phobias won't make them disappear; they need to be addressed with professional counseling.

The first time I experienced fear that took over my entire body was in the middle of the night when my husband was away on a business trip in 1984. I woke up with my heart racing and I was sure our house was on fire. I tried to climb out of bed and discovered I had no feeling in my legs—they collapsed under me. Fear had gripped my body to such an extent that my legs felt para-lyzed, my heart was racing, and I was in a cold sweat from head to toe. I crawled to my children's bedrooms and tried to scream at them to "get out of the house, it is on fire." The only noise that came out of my throat was a raspy, irrational sound and my fear became ever greater with the added feeling of helplessness. I soon realized the house was not on fire, but I was awake for the rest of the night agonizing over the discovery of such intense, helpless, numbing fear.

Fear is complicated and causes unnecessary struggles and perplexity. Before we can stop it, we need to be able to identify it. In the book *Freedom From The Grip of Fear*, the author H. Norman Wright defines fear this way: "Fear is also like a videotape continually replaying our most haunting expe-riences: embarrassing moments, rejections, failures, hurts and disappoint-ments. The message of the fear video is clear: life is full of these experiences, and they *will* repeat themselves. Fear causes us to say, 'I can't do it; I may fail.' It's a constant sense of living in the grip of fear."[61]

It is a proven fact that we are all afraid of something. It is also true that fear will be with us until the day we die; we will never be rid of it. But I have encouraging news; fear does not have to consume or overwhelm us. This chapter focuses on the slavish fear that stops us from reaching our God-given purpose and potential.

What Are You Afraid Of?

If I were to ask you a simple question, "What do you want to be the moti-vating factor in your decision-making: love or fear?" You would say, "Of course it would be love."

Then why are we afraid:

- Of losing control?
- To stop being a perfectionist?
- To love ourselves the way we are?
- To be vulnerable?
- To admit our mistakes?

- To risk adventure?
- That we will never be good enough?
- To forgive ourselves?
- To let disappointments and resentments go?
- To throw off all that hinders us in our spiritual pursuits?
- To fail?

We are afraid because every day we confront the unknown: a new misapprehension. David Foster, in his book *The Power to Prevail*, described fear this way, "It paralyzes your imagination and disengages your will. Fear can rob you of your self-respect. It is like a bottomless pit or a raging storm in which everything gets swallowed up, never to be heard from again."[62]

Missed Opportunities

All of this started over a piece of fruit. Adam and Eve had a perfect relationship with God; He was their Creator, companion and friend. It was the kind of love relationship you and I are looking for, being unconditionally accepted for who we are. One day they deliberately and intentionally chose to disobey God and eat this fruit from the tree of life. They did the one and only thing He told them not to do. When God asked them about it, Adam responded this way. "He answered, 'I heard you in the garden, and I was afraid because I was naked; so I hid'" (Gen. 3:10, NIV). After they disobeyed God's directive to them, they saw themselves for who they really were: disobedient and naked. Fear entered their hearts. We've been afraid ever since, running and hiding from anything that will show our nakedness, weakness, incompetence and sin.

Does this mean that we are fearful because we are weak, and that we can conquer it by simply bucking up, pulling up our bootstraps and "just getting over it?"

It's not that simple and God knows that we struggle with fear every day. The words "fear and feared" are recorded 573 times in the King James

Version of the Bible, and the phrase "fear not" is listed 172 times in the Amplified version. He promises that He will be with us in everything.

I am someone who hates to waste time and miss great opportunities. I never want fear to stop me from grabbing on to those things that have the ability to light my passion, help me to grow stronger and experience God's wonderful gifts to me. I do not want to live with regrets.

I imagine that is why I get so frustrated when I read the parable of the talents. This is a story about a man going on a journey, and entrusting his servants to look after his property. To one servant He gives five talents, to the other servant two talents and to another one He gives one talent—each according to their ability. Wow, what an opportunity. This was a lot of money. The value of a talent in those days was about the lifetime of wages for an average worker. One denarius was about one day's wages, and there were 10,000 denarii in one talent. That's about thirty-five years of wages for one man.

Time passes and the master comes back from his trip and is eager to see what his servants have done with that money. The first servant doubled his five talents, the second servant also doubled his two, but look what happened to the third man; he actually went and buried the money in the ground. When the master confronted him about his talents he said, "I knew that you are a hard man, harvesting where you have not sown and gathering where you have not scattered seed. So I was afraid and went out and hid your talent in the ground" (Matt. 25:24-25, NIV). The master was furious, called him a lazy servant and actually gave his one talent to the one who already had ten talents.

"So I was afraid." Fear caused this lazy servant to lose out on an opportunity for God to double what had been given to him. Jesus talks about giving us opportunities to live with passion and excitement and to experience the joy of discovering what God has given us. Each one of us is loaded with unique abilities, gifts and opportunities and when we learn how to use them for the servicing of God's Kingdom, we reap joy and satisfaction, regardless of how much or little recognition we receive.

Fear Stops Us from Receiving God's Best

I have never met a woman who has not desperately wanted someone to validate her gifts and abilities to be used in fulfilling her God-given purpose and achieving something of value.

I believe that many of us desire to achieve greatness—whether it is big or small. We want the world to notice that we are not part of the mundane, seemingly meaningless daily grind. We have an inner stirring that beckons us to do something significant—and we yearn to know what that is. Often when we discover it, we are too afraid to pursue it. Carol Kent in her book *Tame Your Fears* says:

> Much of our fear centers on being unable to identify what will bring a sense of purpose, joy and fulfillment to our lives. Fear of making the wrong choice in our life's work. Fear of getting trapped in dead-end marriages and or/ vocations. Fear of not knowing how to handle success. Fear of not being fulfilled when everyone says we are successful. Fear of trying something new because we've never succeeded in the past.[63]

It is ever sadder when we discover what fulfills us and gives us joy, but then find we are too fearful to pursue it. Fear almost stopped me from following my passion of teaching women biblical truths so that they could realize their full potential. This desire made my heart pound, kept me awake at night dreaming and planning. I was sure God was using my gifts and abilities to inspire other women and teach them the word of God through speaking to them at conferences and retreats.

At first it felt safe and comfortable because I started speaking to small groups where I was known, welcomed and where we had great interaction. Then came my first opportunity to speak to a large group of women. Fear came knocking at my door in such a powerful way it took me by complete surprise. The night before the conference I hardly slept and got up lightheaded and nauseated. While I was taking my shower I thought I would pass out with the fear of being a failure in front of all those women.

I realized I was creating a chimera and those images were not from God, but I felt helpless to overcome them. I knew there was an enemy trying to stop me and I needed to be careful how I was going to react to this fear. "Be careful—watch out for attacks from Satan, your great enemy. He prowls around like a hungry, roaring lion, looking for some victim to tear apart" (1 Peter 5:8, TLB). I knew in my spirit that I was struggling with a supernatural enemy that was trying to stop me from exercising the gifts God had given me.

Fortitude Takes Action

Then a righteous anger rose up in my spirit and I starting declaring out loud, "I will not succumb to this fear any longer. I am done with it. I refuse to yield to an enemy that wants to rob me from receiving God's best for my life, and for the lives of other women. No longer will I acknowledge or give in to this horrible fear. I am done with the sleepless nights! I am finished with the nausea, and I choose to go out in fortitude and joy." I came out of the shower with new energy and determination. All weekend as I spoke and looked into the eyes of the women in the audience, I was completely without fear. Instead I experienced the most incredible joy and freedom. I chose to look at fear for what it was: an illusion. By challenging it and facing it head on, it shrank to nothing.

God has put us on this earth to build and manage His Kingdom by loving and helping each other. How and where will we find the power and determination to overcome our fear that continually wants to rob our energy and stop us from fulfilling God's purposes?

Overcoming Fear

The Bible tells us, "There is no fear in love. But perfect love drives out fear, because fear has to do with punishment. The one who fears is not made perfect in love" (1 John 4:18, NIV). Let's break that down and see how it applies to you and me.

Fear has to do with punishment. Since Adam and Eve sinned and were punished for their disobedience, we continue to cower, waiting for our punishment. In this present century we could consider our punishment to be that we will get sick; that our house will burn down; that we will go bankrupt; that our children will be killed; that our faults will be exposed. My husband and I always ask ourselves "What is the worst thing that can happen here?" We constantly have to remind ourselves that God has forgiven us for our past sins, He is our provider and protector, and He will take care of whatever happens in the future. God is not out to punish us. He is always ready to fill us with love and waits for us to call out to Him for help. He is not our enemy waiting to punish us; He is our protector and provider.

One who fears is not made perfect in love. We are afraid because on this side of heaven we are incapable of giving and receiving love in its purest form. We don't understand the kind of love that moves us through our time on earth with a perfect purpose. We can't see the future the way God does; so we are afraid of what is around the bend in the road.

But perfect love drives out fear. That powerful little three-letter word, "but," changes the course of our thinking. It acknowledges that we are fearful, *but* God's perfect love can move us beyond that fear. It reminds us that God's love is perfect and nothing will ever be able to separate us from it. Can our minds even comprehend this kind of promise?

"For I am convinced that neither death nor life, neither angels nor demons, neither the present nor the future, not any powers, neither height nor depth, nor anything else in all creation, will be able to separate us from the love of God that is in Christ Jesus our Lord" (Romans 8:38-39, NIV). The more we grasp this kind of love, the greater our fortitude will be to stop our pounding hearts and step into the unknown.

David Foster in his book *The Power to Prevail* puts it this way: "But the most important thing we know about fear is that God wills us to overcome it, not be overcome by it."[64]

Choose the Solution

One size does not fit all when it comes to fear. Harriet Lerner in her book

The Dance of Fear makes this statement: "We all struggle to find the right balance between our human need for security, comfort and predictability on the one hand, and our need for risk taking and growth on the other. In finding this balance, no single formula fits all—or even fits a particular individual over time."[65]

It is ridiculous to assume that any of us would intentionally choose fear. However, when we submit to our fears, they continue to grow. Ultimately we have to change the thought pattern that has been burned into our brain. We have to continually focus on the solution, not the problem. In the story of Peter walking on the water (Matt. 14:22-31) we see what happens when we take our eyes off the end result. In verse 29 Jesus tells Peter, "'Come,' he said. Then Peter got down out of the boat, walked on the water and came toward Jesus. But when he saw the wind, he was afraid and, beginning to sink, cried out, 'Lord, save me!'" As soon as Peter took his eyes off Jesus, he became overwhelmed with the size of the waves, lost focus and fear showed up.

Fortitude Changes the World

By our acts of fortitude we can save lives and change the world. Todd Beamer chose courage when terrorists hijacked United Flight 93 on September 11, 2001. In a recorded phone conversation with a telephone operator just before he took action, Todd said the Lord's Prayer and then gave a command that will go down in history. "Let's roll" were words of fortitude that cause many of us to hold our breath as we try to imagine ourselves in the same circumstances. In the book *Let's Roll*, Lisa Beamer wrote these noble words, "On September 11, 2001, Todd Beamer completed his time on earth. His life ended while 'daring greatly.' He did not die with 'the cold and timid souls who know neither victory or defeat.'"[66]

Todd was willing to die so that many other people could live. In Grace Fox's book *Moving from Fear to Freedom*, she tells about a love that is willing to die for us. "Believing that God is love and that His love extends to us despite our sinfulness is the first step toward rising above our fears. Why? Because knowing the intensity of His love for us allows us to release our worries and rest in His care. If someone loves us so much that He's willing to die on our behalf, we know we can trust Him implicitly regardless of what happens."[67]

I don't know if I will be able to change the world, but I know this: my God knows my life from conception to eternity and I trust Him to help me navigate through the fears that stop me from fulfilling my life's purpose. I also know that God is the essence of love and that even though I will not be protected from my fears, God will help me through them, and be with me in them. I believe in God's promise, "When you pass through the waters, I will be with you; and when you pass through the rivers, they will not sweep over you. When you walk through the fire, you will not be burned; the flames will not set you ablaze. For I am the Lord, your God, the Holy One of Israel, your Savior" (Isa. 43:2-3, NIV).

These promises have helped me to embrace fear as my friend and to find the greatest adventures and joys. Speaking to women and teaching them God's truths is a pleasure and delight I would have missed out on if I had let fear trap me. I have been able to experience adventure with my family by climbing Mount Wengen in Switzerland, climbing the steps of the Eiffel tower in Paris, zooming down the zip line at Rockridge Canyon, British Columbia, white water rafting on the Flathead River in Montana, riding my bike with my grandson over all thirty-six trestles and climbing the highest lighthouse in Poland.

Fear gives us disguised opportunities to discover gifts and joys that God wants to give us. When we see fear as a friend, we will be able to make choices that embrace a whole new way of thinking for us. I encourage you to find the people, words and places that will inspire and empower you to act with fortitude, not fear.

Choices That Enrich Your Life

1. When your job is a boring, endless pit, or when it consumes your waking hours and ruins your family time—choose to quit. There are other jobs better suited for you and your family.

2. When you are being abused in a relationship, choose to seek help and walk away from the abuse.

3. When your beliefs separate you from your family, church, friends or workplace, choose to think for yourself and speak up.

4. Don't be afraid of confusion. Choose to use it as an opportunity to sit and wait for clarity. Don't make irrational decisions just to get comfortable quickly.

5. Don't always give in to instant gratification to feel better in the moment. Your fear is that you will miss out in the future. Choose to wait for something better.

6. Fear of dying is a great motivator to change the course of your thinking. Choose to make this fear a friend that will teach you to take better care of your body, have regular doctor checkups and examine your spiritual life. It can also be a friend to make sure your relationships are in good order and that you are not harboring any unforgiveness.

7. The fear of failure can stop your motivation to pursue excellence. Choose to give your best to everything that God has placed in your life.

8. When you are fearful about your retirement, selling your home, buying a new car or anything that is unknown, choose to search out facts. When you bring facts into the light, you know what you are dealing with and it diminishes fear and moves you to action.

9. The horrible fear of rejection can be used to help you make good choices. Choose to go on a path of personal discovery of your insecurities and find what it is about your personality and character that is making people reject you.

10. When you feel controlled by other people, choose to accept responsibility for every aspect of your life and establish strong boundaries. Choose to stop living in the fear that other people are controlling your life.

11. Discover the things that bring you energy and joy. Choose to eliminate those things that sabotage your pathway to joy.

12. Choose to accept the fact that we will be fearful as long as we live in this human body of flesh and bones with a sinful nature.

13. Choose to realize that life is full of negative things that might happen. Natural disasters will come, because that is part of nature's plan. People will die. Choose to focus on God's love, the love that will be with you through every difficult event you encounter. Choose to believe that nothing can ever separate you from this amazing love.

Stop and Ask God To Help You Change Sand to Pearls

Begin by asking: God, what am I afraid of?

S Scripture: "For God did not give us a spirit of timidity, but a spirit of power, of love and of self-discipline" (2 Tim. 1:7, NIV).

T Thanksgiving: Thank You, God, that You have given me everything that I need to overcome fear. Thank You that You promise to be with me and to help me be an overcomer, and not be overcome by fear.

O Observation: I now realize that fear is not something that I can get rid of by "pulling up my bootstraps" or seeing it as a weakness in my life. I know I need self-discipline to recognize fear and make it my friend so that it will empower me and not diminish me.

P Prayer: Thank You, God, that Your love is pure and powerful, and will help me to overcome fear in my life. Show me how this works when I am so overcome by fear that I lose my rational thinking and succumb to the emotional ravages it can do to my mind and body. Give me the godly wisdom and insight to recognize it and choose fortitude to see it as an opportunity to learn, grow and find more joy. Help me not miss out on adventures and opportunities You want to give me so that I can live the abundant life You have offered to me. Thank You that You are so patient with me as I listen and learn what You want me to experience. Thank You that You have a plan for my life and I pray that I will not let fear stand in the way of reaching my full potential of all that You have created me to be. Please be the source of my pleasure and source of power as I live the daily struggle of knowing who You are and who I am.

Amen.

Chapter 10

Regrets or Rejoicing
A Butterfly Legacy

*There are only two lasting bequests we can
give our children… one is roots, the other wings.*

—STEVEN COVEY

My son Donovan adjusted his Santa hat, took a sip
of his strong morning coffee and made our family's
traditional Christmas morning announcement. "Ok
guys," he said, "this is how it works. We open one present at a time, so that
we all get to watch and appreciate everyone's gifts." My heart started to beat
with excitement and anticipation; I had been planning and waiting for this
moment an entire year. When I sensed that the time was right, I brought
out five flat packages wrapped in shimmering fabric and tied with a big,
gold bow. Finally, there was a lull in the frantic activities, and it was my
turn to make my special presentation.

I handed a flat package to each of my children and stepchildren and
eagerly waited for them to start the unwrapping. Then I described what
was about to happen. "For the last year," I explained, "I have secretly been
accumulating historical pictures and dates of births, deaths and marriages
for both our families and compiling them into a book. I wrote thirty-six
stories about members of our family, so that we can remember and cherish

their uniqueness, their qualities, the laughter and the tears. I desire this book to be part of our family legacy. I want to make sure that our history and these amazing stories will be passed down through the generations; and that the people we love so dearly will never be forgotten." Then I stopped and watched them tenderly open their packages and start reading the first page, the introduction. With tears in my eyes I savored each moment as they lovingly flipped through the pages of my book, called *Looking Back and Enjoying the View*.

Every word in that book was a piece of my heart. I was passionate about passing a legacy of love and grace to the people I love more than anything in this world; my family. I spent an entire year at my computer retracing my life's steps, many times crying so hard I had to stop because I couldn't see the computer screen. I realized that we all have creation stories that need to be passed down through the generations. Through the twists and turns of laughter, sorrow, joy and struggles, God had shaped my life into a beautiful masterpiece. Like the metamorphosis of a butterfly, God used the things that caused me the greatest pain and crushed me into the ground to ultimately give me the greatest joy and make me beautiful from the inside out. Looking back it became crystal clear that not a single moment of my life was wasted; there was nothing that I needed to regret. But I didn't always feel that way.

Metamorphosis of a Legacy

1. Stage One—Caterpillar

After many of my speaking events, women come up to me and bemoan the fact that they have regrets about how their life has turned out. They look at me and perceive a well-dressed, confident woman, one who loves the Lord, and in spite of the struggles I have encountered, life seems to have turned out beautifully—like some kind of magical fairy tale. Many women have so many regrets:

- "I don't have enough education, and now it's too late."
- "I feel that God has overlooked my gifts and abilities, and I've never had an opportunity to use them."

- "I'm too fat or too thin, and it has sabotaged opportunities for a career or other opportunities."
- "I have never been able to build good relationships."
- "I am too old to write a book or start a speaking career."
- "I wasted my life in a bad marriage."
- "If you knew all the bad things I have done in my life, you would see why there is no hope for my life ever becoming beautiful."
- "I've had too much bitterness and I have pushed everyone away from me. It's too late to rebuild those relationships."

I understand and empathize with all of those statements, because I felt as though I wasted the first thirty-two years of my life. But, I have seen how God has used every failure, disappointment, lack of education, every heartache and turned it into something valuable. I truly believe that every tear I have shed has been a seed that was meant to grow and reap new joy. God's ability to restore life is beyond our comprehension, but I know that He is able to bring good out of all our ugliness and tragedies. When I look back I want to shout and dance like the Israelites did when they were released from their Babylonian captivity and returned to their beloved city of Jerusalem. Try to imagine their joy as they sang and danced in the streets: "Those who sow in tears will reap with songs of joy. He who goes out weeping, carrying seed to sow, will return with songs of joy, carrying sheaves with him" (Psalm 126:5-6, NIV).

Not only were they filled with joy, they were carrying provisions that God provided for them to start their new life.

When I look back at my life, I could easily be immersed with sadness and regret. I was incredibly skinny when I was young; my lips were too big for my face and my knees were too big for my thin legs. Not only that, but our family immigrated from Germany, and the first few years in Canada, we were extremely poor and other children made fun of my clothes and my foreign accent. I felt as though I had never really belonged anywhere, like a puzzle piece that just never quite fit.

In spite of our tumultuous circumstances, it was obvious that my parents wanted the very best for our family. Every Sunday we got dressed in our best clothes and trudged off to church. Through my limited understanding I perceived a God that was harsh, judgmental, and it seemed that He was just waiting for me to do something wrong so that He could punish me.

I felt I was being manipulated to have a personal relationship with that God. Adults don't always realize that teenagers are very observant and I could not be fooled into believing something that didn't make sense to me. Why would I want to have a relationship with someone who wanted to punish me, and not accept me for who I was? This confusion of conflicting beliefs caused me to become very rebellious, and I pushed the limits of all the rules in my family and church. They couldn't make me believe that, "This is good, this is bad, this is black and this is white, this is right and this is wrong." I simply refused to comply and cave into their confined ideas, and at eighteen I set out to the big city of Vancouver, British Columbia, to do life "my way." I became the prodigal daughter who left everything behind to find the better life.

That "better life" consisted of living the carefree and exciting lifestyle of the late sixties and early seventies. Even though I tried to convince myself that I was living the good life, I was in fact desperately trying to find my worth, my purpose, and looking for love and trying to be beautiful in all the wrong ways. Through the exhausting process of trying to find the meaning of life my own way, I was really nothing more than a caterpillar crawling through the dirt, pretending I could create my own wings so that I could fly. If I had stayed in this caterpillar stage for the rest of my life I know I would have been consumed with failure and regret. Eventually I became so tired of crawling through a difficult marriage, trying to raise my two beautiful children while my husband was traveling; I entered into a period of deep darkness. During this period the "D" word came up, and yes it was the divorce word. But for me there is a "D" word that is even more debilitating than divorce, and that is the word "despair."

Despair is a dark, empty, hopeless void where we desperately hope for a good forecast for that day, but it always says the same thing: "No Hope Ahead." In many of our caterpillar lives there comes a period in our journey that is so dark, filled with regrets, sorrow and hopelessness, that whether we believe in a God or not, we still cry out in anguish, "God, help me!" That honest, gut-wrenching wail is always heard by God, and He always answers. This is the pivotal spot where the most dramatic life transformation stage takes place—from a caterpillar to the chrysalis.

For me that change happened with one word; grace.

2. Stage Two—Chrysalis

This is a state in our lives where nothing seems to be happening; yet *everything is changing.*

After I cried, *"God help me!"* He brought a beautiful family into our family's life. They became our best friends and we did everything together except for one thing: every Sunday they went to church. Each week they kindly asked all of us to go with them, but we always responded, "No thank you." Nothing or no one was going to drag me back into a church. Eventually, though, there comes a time when we either walk off the dark edge of despair or we grab the lifeline that God throws us. Finally I was drained of all hope and energy and was desperate enough to seize the hope that God placed in front of me. I started attending church with my friends, and there I discovered the most amazing, startling revelation. I found God to be a Heavenly Father who had been pursuing me all my life, with arms open wide, and He was just waiting for me to have an intimate, loving relationship with Him. "How great is the love the Father has lavished on us, that we should be called children of God! And that is what we are!" (1 John 3:1, NIV).

I longed for someone to lavish love on me, and I desired to know that I really belonged to someone who would accept me for who I was, dirt and all. In this amazing love experience I found a word that defies human understanding: "grace." This word began my supernatural heart transformation from being a lost soul looking for purpose and meaning face down in the dirt to looking up to God and learning how to be free and fly. This transformation started in my head, by learning that grace is a free, unmerited gift given to me by God, that it forgives me for all my past sins and loves me today just the way I am. Then I had to accept this truth in my heart and let it begin to transform my wounded, broken and insecure soul. I often say to women, "Learning God's truth is the longest journey of my lifetime; it is the journey from my head to my heart."

The Bible tells us, "Don't copy the behavior and customs of this world, but let God transform you into a new person by changing the way you think. Then you will learn to know God's will for you, which is good and pleasing and perfect" (Rom. 12:2, NLT). It's so hard to imagine that by making a choice to accept God's grace our lives will be changed dramatically—albeit slowly, one courageous, trusting step of faith at a time.

To let go of a life of regrets, I had to first of all extend that word "grace" to myself. I hear many people say that "our past is our past" and to leave well enough alone. But I believe that we are only good today to the degree that we have dealt with our past. Our former life is the one that has shaped us, developed our habits, thinking patterns and perception of the world around us. If we do not give grace to ourselves to accept our past, forgive all the people who have hurt us, and forgive ourselves, we will never be transformed into a new person.

Gordon MacDonald is also a great believer of dealing with our past. He says, "We carry within ourselves all our yesterdays, the experiences and influences that have happened from our birth (and maybe before) to this present moment. These yesterdays can powerfully affect us *today*—the right now—and dominate our relationships, our choices, our views of ourselves, even our understanding of God. If our yesterdays are in a state of good repair, they provide strength for today. If not repaired, they create havoc."[68]

Grace gave me the power to forgive the people who had hurt me in my past, including my husband, my father, pastors in the churches that had made me angry, teachers who had treated me badly and friends who had excluded me when I so desperately wanted to belong. It also gave me permission and courage to rip the duct tape off all my mistakes and failures and instead see them as stepping stones to acquire wisdom. How foolish of me to think that I could cover and protect my wounded and insecure heart and hope that no one would ever see how broken I was.

This word "grace" impacted my life so profoundly that I want it to be the influencing power in every area of my life, today and beyond. The word "grace" in the Greek language is *charis*,[69] the root word of *chara*, which is described as, "joy, and delight, akin to rejoice".[70] In order for me to let go of regrets and choose to rejoice, I must apply grace to every area of my life, especially to the people I love most—my family—and all my areas of influence. I want to be an influencer and grow beautiful grace wings just like Naomi did in the story of Ruth.

3. Stage Three—Magnificent Wings

Every time I read the story of Naomi, I feel that she and I have a kindred heart. The story starts out in the book of Ruth, about a family in Bethlehem, a husband, wife and two sons. There was a famine in the land, so one day the father came home and told the family they were moving to the strange, foreign land of Moab.

As I read this, I can vividly remember my husband Dick coming home one day in 1992 and saying, "Honey, we have to move to Kelowna, British Columbia." I realize that Kelowna is one of the most beautiful regions in Canada, but in reality, our family had made their home in Lethbridge, Alberta for thirteen years; and the idea of moving anywhere else was immediately traumatic. But, Naomi and her family moved to Moab. Dick and Heidi moved to Kelowna, British Columbia.

The story goes on to say, "And they went to Moab and lived there. Now Elimelech, Naomi's husband, died" (Ruth 1: 2-3, NIV). Boom, dead; just like that. No fanfare, no explanation. Naomi is left alone in a distant, alien land with her two sons, who in the meantime married Moab women. The story goes on to say, "They married Moabite women, one named Orpah and the other Ruth. After they had lived there about ten years, both Mahlon and Kilion also died, and Naomi was left without her two sons and her husband" (Ruth 1:4-5, NIV). More tragedy! Now Naomi is all alone in this unfamiliar country, except for her two Moabite daughters-in-law.

After Dick and I moved to Kelowna, he died playing basketball, and I was left alone in an unfamiliar city. Here is where my heart connects with Naomi, because both of us have lost our husbands and we are left to fend for ourselves in an alien place. Something transpired in Naomi's life in the ten years that her sons were married to Moabite women that makes me sit up and take intense notice. I know how hard it was to be a widow in 1994, and yet there was almost nothing worse than being a widow in the ancient world; widows were either taken advantage of or ignored. Even though the story does not explain this ten-year period where Naomi is a widow and mother-in-law to Moabite women, she must have endured it with unusual grace and tenacious strength and faith in her God. When Naomi decided to go back to her beloved Bethlehem, her daughter-in-law Ruth said to her, "Don't urge me to leave you or to turn back from you. Where you go I will go, and where you stay I will stay. Your people will be my people and your God my God. Where you die I will die" (Ruth 1:16-17, NIV). Every time I read this I stand amazed, humbled, and ponder about what must have transpired in their relationship for Ruth to plead with Naomi to let her come along and to let "your God be my God." I surmise that it can only be *grace.*

Women can be harsh, critical and competitive, especially when it comes to differences in "the way we do things." Naomi must have accepted her daughter-in-law's foreign culture, the different foods, the way she dressed, the way she spoke, shopped, cleaned her home, and the way she treated her son. I can only speculate that Naomi also modeled that her God was a god of comfort and strength during her intense grieving process for her husband and two sons and struggling to survive as a widow. Grieving is not pretty, and it can bring out our worst fears and emotions. So I see no other explanation for one woman to say to another, "I will follow you wherever you go." It can only be grace.

It was gorgeous grace that melted my crusty heart and drew me into the loving, accepting arms of God. I believe it is only grace that has the undeniable power to break down all barriers and pull off all our duct tape, so that we can reveal our hearts to each other and have the courage to accept each other just the way we are. "Accept other believers who are weak in faith, and don't argue with them about what they think is right or wrong" (Rom. 14:1, NLT). I choose to pour out God's gorgeous, tender yet powerful grace on everyone that I meet by accepting them for exactly who they are at that moment. It is my desire that by doing this they will see a reflection of God's beauty through me and be able to say, "Heidi, I choose to let your God become my God." When we choose to saturate our life with God's grace, we reflect the beauty of God's glory and splash it onto everyone we meet.

Kerry and Chris Shook give us these captivating facts about butterflies: "I find it fascinating that the coloring on a butterfly is not caused by pigment but rather by a prism-like effect as light is reflected off its transparent wings. Despite the variety of colors and patterns, beneath the arrangement of their wing design, all butterfly wings are transparent. Similarly, in our lives, transparency transforms. When we get real with God and others, when we're being who God created us to be rather than trying to pretend we're someone else, then our distinct beauty emerges."[71] Before we know it, the duct tape comes off and releases our beautiful, prism-like wings. We're ready to fly.

Regret or Rejoice?

I have found it to be true that my greatest power to love and help other people has emerged from my deepest pain, shame and failures. God has taken it all and turned it around into beauty that I believe will transcend this generation. I can confidently say that all my regrets have turned into rejoicing:

- I never felt smart enough. Even though my parents did not believe I should have education beyond grade twelve, I have been able to establish a successful career, and a writing and international speaking ministry. God answers me when I pray, "God make me smarter than I am."

- I always felt I did not measure up with my physical appearance. God has helped me to become beautiful on the inside, which makes me feel accepted and beautiful on the outside.

- God helped me clean up my box of guilt and shame. Nancie Carmichael talks extensively about this in her book, *Surviving One Bad Year*, and says, "Guilt, anger and shame can be so deeply ingrained in our hearts that they color everything in our lives, and we're not even aware they are there. But they weigh us down and keep us from joyfully running the race God has set before us."[72] When God helped me empty the junk in my boxes, I began to feel free to soar.

- Disappointment has turned into acceptance. I realized that God made me this way for a purpose and that I will never achieve perfection, but that I can rejoice because I am uniquely made and I am "perfect in Him."

- God taught me to deal with unfairness. People and circumstances in this world may be unfair, but God is always fair. If I am going to be a reflection of His beauty, then in spite of how the world treats people, it is up to me to treat everyone with fairness. This has been a huge step in helping me to see the world through eyes of compassion, not unfairness.

I know for a fact that God can take all our regrets and turn them into rejoicing. How can I be so adamant about this? Because God is the Creator of everything, and everything He created can be restored by Him. There is only one obstacle that you and I need to overcome; we need to *choose to let Him do it. What we choose determines where the rest of us goes.*

The chrysalis stage is where our life's struggles are transformed into beauty and joy. We cannot short-circuit this stage or try to hurry it up; we have to allow God to transform us in His time and His way. Forget about trying to become a "new you in a mere twenty-one days." Becoming beautiful and turning our regrets into rejoicing takes time, sometimes much longer than we think. There is a story about a young boy who tried to help a butterfly emerge from its chrysalis. He took out a little pocketknife to cut the chrysalis and release the butterfly to eliminate some of its struggle. As he pulled out the butterfly and held it in his hands, he expected it to fly away, but instead it died. We live in a generation where we have ways to speed up practically anything, but if we want to flourish and grow our wings, we cannot speed up God's transformation process.

I was privileged to facilitate a study group where we enjoyed a time of learning how to be transformed into a butterfly by being loving and authentic and understanding God's grace. In the last week of our study I asked this question: "What kind of a legacy do you want to leave?" These were some their answers:

- Twyla said, "The legacy that I'd like to be remembered for is *time*. That my family and friends would feel that I always had *time* for them. That I was never too busy."
- Arlene said, "I want my tombstone to read, 'She lived her life with no regrets'."
- Lorraine said, "Restore hope for the greater dream in the lives of others."
- Larry said, "To live with integrity."
- Beth said, "To know that some things are worth fighting for."
- Marlene said, "Time and Love."

As we finished our discussions on leaving a legacy, and turning regrets into rejoicing, I gave them more good news. Not only does God turn our regrets into rejoicing, He can choose to double our portion of that which we feel has been lost. "Instead of their shame my people will receive a double portion, and instead of disgrace they will rejoice in their inheritance; and so they will inherit a double portion in their land, and everlasting joy will be theirs" (Isa. 61:7, NIV).

That's what God's grace does—it gives us everlasting joy—and when we begin to pour it out onto the rest of the world, it changes lives wherever we go.

Not too long ago I watched the enthralling production of *CNN Heroes* (2009). As I sat there with a box of Kleenex, I marveled at the astounding endeavors taken by ordinary people, to bring food for the homeless, medical care for the poor, wheelchairs for the broken bodies, and building homes for children who lost their parents. At the end of the presentations the winner said these compelling words, "Inside of each of us there is a hero. We just need to find him and unleash him."

I started my legacy for my family by writing a book and presenting it to them on Christmas morning. Since that time, the word "legacy" has kindled a passion that compels me to try to live each day with intention and grace. Each of us has an area of influence where we have the potential to do something profound that will leave a valuable footprint on this earth. I also believe that inside of each of us is a story of a gorgeous butterfly legacy. It is up to you to find it and unleash it so that it can fly.

Choices That Enrich Your Life

1. You look around at the younger women and see that they have exciting careers and are not stuck in the house like you were when you were raising your children. Choose to believe that God had *your* purpose for *your* life in that time of the history of the world. Perhaps now is your opportunity to do something exciting and fulfilling for yourself.

2. You have been stuck in a meaningless, dull marriage and you feel that your life has been wasted. Choose to believe that nothing is wasted if we allow God to use our pain and transform it into something worthwhile. Today you can start by doing something worthwhile outside of your home to make a difference in your local neighborhood, nursing home, library or food bank. When we begin to bring joy into other people's lives, it will start to splash back on us.

3. You are heartbroken because you have never been able to have children. You look around at families and regret that you never took the time or courageous effort to adopt a child from another country.

Choose today to start mentoring a younger woman, a teenager, or immerse yourself in teaching younger children in Sunday school or supervising at your local elementary school. I have a very dear, unmarried friend who at the age of forty-five adopted a child from Ethiopia. It has transformed regrets into incredible, endless joy.

4. You look back at your life and realize you have been stuck in a hollow, dull job most of your life. Choose to believe that your one and only life should be lived with passion and meaning and it is *never too late* to discover your strengths and start doing something you love. Remember, a fruitful life is not about money, but about finding your purpose and making a difference in this world.

5. You look back and realize you should have invested more money to prepare for your retirement. Perhaps that is true, but what is right now is what you have to work with. Each one of us came into this world naked, and we leave with one outfit on our bodies. Choose to believe that if God takes care of the sparrows and the lilies of the field, He will take care of you. Choose to believe that God is a God of abundance, not poverty, and that when you pray and ask Him to help you, He will.

6. Your life has been filled with bitterness and anger towards your family. Choose to ask God to help you forgive your family, and to forgive yourself so that you can turn all regrets into rejoicing. (See Epilogue for Steps to Forgiveness.)

7. I had a fifty-year-old woman tell me how much she regretted never writing the book that she felt God had written on her heart. I excitedly told her that it is never too late to write a book and that she had until the rest of her life to do it but today was probably a good day to start.

8. You had an abortion when you were younger and you simply cannot get over that regret of taking a life. You've tried to forgive yourself but nothing seems to take the shame and guilt away. Choose today to believe that God's *gorgeous grace* has removed that sin and pain

as far as the east is from the west. Today, look for a counselor or agency that will help you walk through your grieving stages for this lost child. You will never be able to fly until you have given this pain to God.

9. You missed out on an opportunity to be married and today you are still single. You regret that you let that opportunity slip by. Choose to believe that God's timing is always perfect and perhaps this man was not ready for you, or you were not ready for him. Choose to live your life passionately and fully until God brings that man into your life who will be just right for you.

10. You regret the way you raised your children. It is never too late to humbly ask your children for forgiveness. Choose to start treating them differently with the new insights that God has given you.

11. A divorced father told me how much he regretted alienating his children during the time of his divorce. After I talked to him about the butterfly legacy, he made a choice that day to start calling his children and do whatever it took to start the reconciliation process. He chose to change his regrets into rejoicing.

12. I had an eighty-year-old woman tell me how she had regrets about not having a speaking platform when she was younger. Even though she realizes this was not something that women did at the time of her younger years, she feels she could have impacted other women through being bold and having a platform. After I discussed this with her for some time she chose to believe that God used her to inspire, nurture and teach women by through the gifts and abilities He gave her for that time in history. She chose to trust God with the way He used her life.

13. Choose to believe that most of our regrets come from some missed opportunity, or events that were painful, sinful or ugly. Choose to trust that most of these regrets will be covered by God's grace and forgiveness, and for the rest trust God that He knew what He was doing with your one and only life.

Stop and Ask God to Help You Change Sand to Pearls

Begin by asking: What regrets are stopping me from living my one and only life with passion and purpose?

S Scripture: "Those who sow in tears will reap with songs of joy. He who goes out weeping, carrying seed to sow, will return with songs of joy, carrying sheaves with him" (Psalm 126:5-6, NIV).

T Thanksgiving: Thank You, God, for the comforting promise that You will replace my weeping with joy. Some days it feels like sadness and sorrow is so heavy that it will never leave. Thank You also that You tell me it will stop. What a wonderful assurance to know that You understand my weeping and that there is hope for "songs of joy." I can hardly wait.

O Observation: You tell us in the Bible that "we reap what we sow." What an incredible encouragement to know that every tear that I have sown over regrets You will one day replace with a new joy. Not only that, but You give me the security of knowing that after my sadness and grieving, You will provide blessings for me that will reenergize me and sustain me in the days to come.

P Prayer: God, You are so kind and good to me. I do not want to live with any regrets in this life; I choose instead to live a life of passion, purpose and rejoicing. Help me to distinguish those areas of regrets where there is unresolved hurt and anger, and where I still need to offer forgiveness to other people and to myself. Help me to replace all unkindness with blessing. God, most of all, I long to experience Your amazing grace in every area of my life, so that I can in turn splash it onto everyone I meet. I have such a hard time understanding Your unconditional kindness, especially for some of the sinful things I have done. Please move the "understanding" of grace from my head to the "experiencing" of grace in the depth of my soul. I long to be the kind of person that looks behind me and sees only the smiling faces of people that I have blessed in this life. I know I cannot do this on my own; I need the infusion and direction of Your Holy Spirit to saturate me with Your grace so that it becomes a part of who I am. Thank You for Your faithfulness, and help me to trust that You can turn all my regrets into rejoicing, that You can replace all my pain and weeping into a newfound joy. I thank You, God, that You love me enough to do this for me.

Amen.

Chapter 11

Shamed or Radiant

Who Do You Want Me To Be?

Shame is often like an atomic particle; we often know where it is only by the trace it leaves, by the effects it causes.

—MICHAEL LEWIS, author

I was blissfully pecking away on my laptop, anticipating our family rushing through our front door at any minute. It was spring break here in Kelowna, and a perfect time for my step-daughter Janice, her husband Ken and my three grandchildren to come for a skiing holiday. I heard the van pull into the driveway and I beat them to the door. With a grin on my face I watched my three blond-headed grandsons come bouncing out of the blue minivan. But wait, there is another boy; they brought a guest.

That Sunday morning as we were getting ready to go to church our phone rang. It was a friend of mine who is a single mother, and a nurse at our hospital. I heard a tired voice at the other end of the line tell me, "Heidi, I have to work overtime, can you please pick Mitchell up and take him to Sunday school with you?"

"Of course, I would be happy to," I said. At the same time I was thinking, *We already have four boys here; how much more trouble can one extra boy be?*

When we got to church we discovered that there would be no Sunday school that day; they decided to give all the teachers a reprieve during spring break. Undeterred, we rounded up all the coloring books, matchbox cars and reading material we could get our hands on and found an empty pew up in the balcony. Once we settled in, I picked up the bulletin and read that our pastor was speaking on the topic of love. Perfect, this would be more research for a conference I was presently working on.

The boys were behaving beautifully. I had my six-year-old grandson Ryan on my right and our visitor friend Mitchell on my left. I could tell Ryan was intently listening to the sermon because halfway through the morning his adorable little face looked over at Mitchell and whispered, "I love my Nana and she loves me!" Mitchell's head bobbed up and he hissed back, "Well I love her, too."

Both heads went back to their coloring, but I could feel a tension in the air. Moments later Ryan demanded more attention by raising his voice one octave louder, "Well, I kiss her all the time and she kisses me back." Mitchell volleyed back with a winning hand by hissing, "Well, she kisses me all the time, and she leaves lipstick marks right here." Mitchell hates those lipstick marks that I would leave on his check from time to time—but today those smudges had become his badge of honor.

I know my little Ryan, he is very competitive and he wasn't done yet. Sure enough, within a few moments he stood up, put his hands on his little hips and shouted, "Well, I'm her grandson!" To which Mitchell yelled back, "Well, I'm going to ask her to marry me!"

They both tried climbing all over me, shoving and pushing for more of my lap territory. We had to separate them and take them out of the sanctuary. The love competition was over. My love research that morning was a real eye-opener. Everybody wants to be a winner.

I Am a Winner

I discovered that no matter how young or old we are, we all need to know that we have value, that we are loved, and that we are known for something.

We have to know that we have an identity worthy and acceptable to the rest of society.

From a small baby screaming for attention, to a young boy in church shouting that he is a favorite grandson, to an adult woman always drawing the conversation to herself; we need the world to know we exist and that we have significance.

The next time the summer or winter Olympics are on TV, take a few days and watch the participants. These young men and women have spent most of their lives preparing for this grueling moment of finding their worth and showcasing it for the whole world. They have sacrificed their time, relationships, finances and sleep for this opportunity to show their friends, family and the world that they are winners. To be a champion and have an Olympic ribbon placed around their necks is the ultimate display of definitive significance.

In the book *Shame: Identity Thief,* Dr. Henry Malone says that "Our needs can be defined in many different terms, but most behavioral scientists agree on certain basic needs of all human beings:

1. We need unconditional love.
2. We need to feel we have intrinsic value.
3. We need to feel a measure of power in our lives.
4. We need to be acknowledged or known.
5. We need an avenue by which we can be heard so that we can feel important.
6. We need to feel we are protected by someone.
7. We need to feel we are understood when we express ourselves.

If these human needs are not met, we receive shame in our spirit and soul."[73]

All those seven needs indicate our desperate need for significance. All of us can remember a time in school when we knew we had the right answer and threw up our hand waiting to share that knowledge. We need people to know that we're not stupid, that we have value, that we are a winner.

The only way we can measure this is to compare ourselves with other people. We realize that we never quite match up to who we were designed to be—or who we think we should be. We know our weaknesses, flaws and ugliness; and it makes us feel emotionally naked, alienated and ashamed. We will do whatever it takes to cover our shame, and without realizing it we create our own identities that will be acceptable to society so that we will get the love and approval we desperately need.

Failure to Thrive

Our souls need love as much as a body needs oxygen to stay alive. We will manipulate and orchestrate our lives so that we get the necessary dose of love for our daily survival. You and I have a choice each day: survive or thrive.

There is a medical diagnosis called FTT, or failure to thrive. John Ortberg explained this in an article in *Christianity Today* in which he explains what his wife Nancy says about this condition, "But of all the diagnoses I ever heard her discuss, FTT is the one that sticks in my mind. Those initials would go on the chart of an infant who, often for unknown reasons, was unable to gain weight or grow."[74]

I see the FTT diagnosis in grown-up men and women who struggle with shame and are unable to acknowledge who they really are and to grow into the person God created them to be. They live each day simply surviving and not thriving—and sadly they believe this is the design for their life. Years of numbing themselves against the onslaught of their sins and failures have convinced them that this is all they deserve.

"Thrive" is a word full of vitality, flourishing and increasing in who we are and the things we do. Surviving is simply shuffling through each day trying to stay alive by enduring the onslaught of our daily struggles.

Right now you have the power to choose which one you would rather do. Sadly, there is an obstacle standing in your way, one that is rarely talked about. Very few books have been written about this topic, and it is hardly ever taught in our churches—it is the menacing power and control of shame.

Where Does Shame Come From?

We live in a success-orientated world with everything at our disposal to create beauty in every area of our lives. We are surrounded and inspired by people and companies that market beauty and success. We are bombarded with images of the most successful career, the best baseball player, the longest bridge, the best student, best author, singer, artist... the list of superlatives is endless. But underneath all this emphasis on striving, most of us walk around knowing we can never hope to live up to the expectations of the world around us. We have nagging doubts about our abilities and our characters, and we hardly ever measure up to the demands of being a perfect ten, airbrushed, slim, gorgeous, perfect mother, employee, wife or friend.

Most of our feelings of being unlovable and unworthy were experienced when we were very young. Sadly they continue to perpetuate themselves in our adult years. We discover we may be ashamed of:

- Having been raised in a poor family or neighborhood.
- Having something done to us that violated our boundaries or body.
- Failure to live up to society's standard of attractiveness and competence.
- Being told we were bad, stupid or being otherwise humiliated.
- Getting older and watching our bodies change.
- Having a mental or physical handicap.
- Feeling like a piece of a puzzle that doesn't fit.
- A prior addiction, abortion or an affair.
- Belonging to the wrong culture or religion.

Shame is rooted and experienced in the exchange between people. Each time we encounter or are reminded of one of our past shameful experiences, our feelings continue to tell us that we are damaged goods. We feel like we don't fit in or belong. We just feel wrong. This may cause us to blush, lower our gaze, bite our tongue or lip, force a smile, fidget, and get angry or withdraw. Shame makes us want to fade into a wall or drop through a crack, whatever it takes to disappear.

I believe that God desires us to see ourselves as beautiful. After all, the essence of God is love and beauty and we are made in His image. We don't see ourselves this way because we are confused and have no idea why. In our hearts we know we were destined for beauty and greatness and yet we suffer and limp from a serious wound.

The Hebrew word for "shame" is *kalam*, "to wound; but only fig., to taunt or insult, be (make) ashamed, blush, be confounded, to be put to confusion, hurt, reproach."[75] Each one of us can remember a time when we were wounded. We can still feel the searing pain that caused us to flinch, cower and ultimately hide. We have been doing this since Adam and Eve disobeyed God and sinned in the Garden of Eden: "I heard you in the garden, and I was afraid because I was naked; so I hid" (Gen. 3:10, NIV). This sinning, shame and hiding has followed and haunted us through the generations.

When I teach on the topic of shame at workshops or conferences, the room becomes very quiet and I can feel the uncomfortable tension of pain. Invariably by the end of the session there is brokenness, and tears fall as women begin to understand the shame they have been carrying and trying to cover up their entire lives. There is also a shock factor when they realize how shame has become part of their identity and how they have been hiding behind false protective masks. It is a painful reality when we realize shame has had this much power and control in our lives.

Masks Hide Our Shameful Identity

When we are running behind schedule we may leave the house with a button missing, a coffee stain or without makeup. We can tolerate this inadequacy once in a while, but what if people could see beyond our imperfect physical condition and look at our insecurities, anger, critical attitude and malicious judgmental thoughts? We know our society urges us to cover up our ugliness. Especially in our churches we want to appear as if we are living a victorious, joyful Christian life.

Believing we are too flawed to be worthy of acceptance in society, we hide by creating our personalized, acceptable masks. When we put on a mask we can be whoever we need to be and anything is possible. We can move and act the way we need to and can be transformed into anything emotional, spiritual or physical that is acceptable in society and that makes us stand out from the many other faces in the crowd.

The dictionary describes masks this way: "A covering for all or part of the face, usually worn to conceal one's identity, false face. Anything that disguises or conceals; a pretense."[76] There is the answer; a mask to cover our flaws and failures so that we are acceptable to society.

Moses, the friend of God who led the Israelites through the wilderness, had an encounter with God on top of Mount Sinai. This left his face glowing and radiant, and he probably felt important. Sadly, when we take our eyes off God or lose the intimacy we have with God, we lose our radiance. That's what happened to Moses: the radiance faded and he covered his face with a veil. The Bible tells it this way: "We are not like Moses, who would put a veil over his face to keep the Israelites from gazing at it while the radiance was fading away" (2 Cor. 3:13, NIV). He didn't want the people to see that he wasn't the super spiritual, glowing, radiant leader anymore. He thought he was fooling people by putting a veil over his face.

You and I are no different; we think we are fooling people by wearing invisible masks. There is a price to pay for wearing masks. They prevent us from experiencing intimacy with God and from knowing ourselves the way God sees us. Let's identify some of our masks so that we can ask God to remove them:

- Perfectionist: "I will earn my love by appearing to be perfect in everything I do."
- Performer: "If I have many accomplishments, I will be admired and loved."
- Pretending Competence: "If I appear smarter than I am, people will respect me."
- Plastic Smile: "If I keep smiling, no one will know I feel overlooked, resentful, angry and like a loser."
- Perfectly Content: "If I appear content, people will think I have God's peace in my life and I won't have to answer probing questions."

- Paying for Guilt: "I owe the world for what I have done—or that which has been done to me."
- Putting Up with Abuse: "I deserve to be punished, because I am guilty."
- People-Pleasing: "I have to orchestrate my life to do whatever people ask of me so that in turn I will receive the love I desperately need."

How sad that so many are going through life playing a role that we were never designed to play. God's radiant beauty within you cannot show through a plastic, painted mask.

Out of Its Secret Box

Shame begins to feel like our underwear; it becomes a daily component of our wardrobe and feels like it belongs to us. Until we look at it, we forget there were things in the past that caused us to feel so different, ugly and ashamed.

I recall the year that I was going into grade seven and didn't have anything new to wear. My mom suggested that I wear a sweater with the buttons in the back instead of the front. "It would be a new look," she said. I can still feel the heat on my cheeks as I compared myself to other students going into grade seven. They looked fashionable and cool, and I felt like a misfit. Loud words echoed in my head that said, "You don't fit in! You don't belong! You are a loser."

When we have a splinter in our finger, break a bone or burn ourselves, it is a message designed to tell us that something is wrong. In the same way, when we take our painful life experiences from the darkness of our secret box, they will begin to shed light on the anguish that propelled us to start wearing protective masks.

There is always a positive and negative avenue for all our feelings. Our magnificent God made us perfect and He gave us our feelings; but we have to be able to differentiate between the ones that will help us and the ones that will hurt us. There are two types of shame.

Circumstantial Shame (False Shame)

This is shame that we accept for inappropriate things. They may have been things we overheard as a child that were too much for our little souls to bear. It may be responsibilities we took on because of other people's wrong choices. Much of our circumstantial shame is something that was thrust upon us and was beyond our control. We may feel shame simply because we are alive and we feel as though we don't belong on this earth. Here are some of the voices we may have heard in our minds:

- "I am responsible for my parent's divorce."
- "I am responsible for my husband's pornography addiction."
- "I should have stopped him from taking that trip."
- "If I had been a better mother, this would not have happened."
- "It's my fault that daddy was so angry all the time."
- "If only I had worked harder... stopped the abuse... listened... been there."

The accusations go on and on. Our condemnation continues to take authority over our thoughts and motivates us to make anemic choices. Whenever we feel failure, we replay the voices in our head.

We may have heard words like, "You idiot, why did you do that?" "Can't you do anything right?" "What is wrong with you?" "Pull yourself together—don't be such a baby." "Stop crying or I will give you something to cry about."

Other people continue to give us shame. In the book *The Dance of Fear* author Harriet Lerner states, "People do give us shame, and they may give generously both at the office and at home. Shame comes from the outside, although by the time we're adults we've internalized so much of it that even a tiny perceived insult from another can rev it up."[77]

This shame that we keep hidden in our secret box will never magically go away or evaporate; it will continue to defile and cripple us.

Sinful Shame (Real Shame)

This shame is a result of guilt of wrongdoing that has not been dealt with. This feeling is meant to drawn us into the loving, redeeming arms of our

Heavenly Father for sorrowful repentance. It is to motivate us and remind us to live a life of honesty, purity and integrity through the powerful act of forgiveness. When we repent of the sin that caused the guilt, our spirits will be free from other people's hooks and our faces will radiate with the beauty of that freedom.

Removing Shame

When I discovered and started to unpack the shame in my own life, I had no idea the power it had over choices that I made. We make choices out of who we believe we are. If our identity is shamed-based, we will make choices that will always protect our sins, failures and inadequacies behind our masks. We may think we are protecting ourselves, but in fact we are sabotaging our chances to live the abundant life that Jesus died for. As long as we keep accusations and debilitating voices in our secret box, they will have power to keep us hiding from people and circumstances that will provoke that feeling of shame.

Jesus scorned shame for you and me. The word "scorned" is defined as "to show contempt for; abhor, despise, detest, loathe, disapprove of, disfavor, considered despised or unworthy, to reject or refuse with derision."[78] The Son of God accepted all people and crossed all social, economical and cultural barriers. He ate with sinners, healed all who touched Him, allowed a sinful woman to pour expensive perfume on His feet, fed the poor, and hung around with tax collectors and lepers.

Jesus was very familiar with shame. He endured it because He knew His purpose and focused on the joy that was beyond the present moment. His friends abandoned Him, He was betrayed by Judas, people accused Him of blasphemy, He was beaten with a whip, taunted, stripped of His clothes and forced to carry His own cross. He had to endure the humiliation of wearing a crown of thorns and watch as men threw dice to see who would get His royal clothes. As He was hanging on the cross waiting to die for our sin, a criminal who hung next to Him hurled insults and mocked Him by shouting, "Aren't you the Christ? Save yourself and us!" (Luke 23:39, NIV).

That is exactly what Jesus did; He saved us. He died so that we would no longer have to carry our shame. "Let us fix our eyes on Jesus, the author and perfecter of our faith, who for the joy set before him endured the cross, scorning its shame, and sat down at the right hand of the throne of God. Consider him who endured such opposition from sinful men, so that you will not grow weary and lose heart" (Heb. 12:2-3, NIV).

Jesus modeled shameless, unconditional love for us. Through this we know that no matter who we are, what we have done or what has been done to us, nothing will have the power to separate us from His love. This kind of love gives us permission to let go of our shame. If we hang on to it, it is like telling Jesus that He died for nothing, that His death has no power in our lives. We need to take refuge in the truth of God's promises that, "Therefore, there is now no condemnation for those who are in Christ Jesus, because through Christ Jesus the law of the Spirit of life set me free from the law of sin and death" (Rom 8:1-2, NIV).

1. Removing Circumstantial Shame (False Shame)

One of the most powerful verses in the Bible to help me with shame is, "I sought the Lord, and he answered me; he delivered me from all my fears. Those who look to him are radiant; their faces are never covered with shame" (Psalm 34:4-5, NIV).

Circumstantial shame is a false shame, and it is a feeling of *being wrong*. The only way to get rid of a feeling is through an action called "surrender." We need to seek God and look to Him to lift our shame from us. Many of us shudder when we hear that word; we all hate to part with something that we've become comfortable with. Let me unleash the word surrender with a different dimension. *When we give something over to God we are giving Him something that has been flawed through our sin; and God can take it and make something beautiful out of it.* When we give our shame to God, we have to understand that we will receive freedom and radiance in return. Katie Brazelton, in her book *Pathway to Purpose for Women*, explains it so well:

We give an offering to God when we surrender, but he gives us far more in return. As we surrender to God, he begins to transform our lives. The result of a transformed life is that we experience the precious blessings of his Spirit: love, joy, peace, patience, kindness, goodness, faithfulness, gentleness and self-control. The more we surrender, the more we are transformed, and the more these blessings flow from the Spirit to us.... If you and I could bottle these things and sell them, we'd be very rich women. Yet God gives them in abundance to women who surrender to him and serve him with their lives.[79]

Here is how to surrender:

a. Ask God to reveal your wounds.

b. Ask Him for the truth of that situation.

c. Choose to surrender by saying, "God, I acknowledge the wound of_____. Please give me the strength to surrender the shame that occurred in this circumstance. I now give it to You, believing that You can remove my shame and restore me with peace and new radiance in my life."

d. Each time the wound reappears, continue to give it to God until you feel the release from the shame.

e. Thank God for sending His Son to die for you so that you could live a forgiven life—free from shame.

f. Wait with eager anticipation to see how God will turn your shame into a newfound freedom and, ultimately, radiance.

It helps me to look back and see that every time I surrendered shame, it gave me courage to step out and make choices that helped me become the unique creation I was designed to be. One of those occasions was an oil painting course that lasted for an entire week. A well-known artist was coming to town, and this was my long-awaited opportunity to get some professional, hands-on painting instructions. I was so excited; I could hardly wait for Monday to arrive. The first day I had a blast and that evening I proudly took home my first painting. Halfway through Tuesday, the artist asked everyone to gather around my painting. I remember my face was blushing because I felt so proud that my painting was chosen as an example of good painting technique. I shall never forget the words out of her mouth, "Let's gather around Heidi's painting, so that I can show you all what *not* to do." I wanted the floor to open up so that I could disappear. My face burned with humiliation and all I wanted to do was take my paintbrushes and leave. Silently I endured the rest of that day but vowed not to go back for the remainder of the course. The artist's words validated my insecurities and shame reminded me that I did not have any creative gifts; that I was worthless, useless, and I felt degraded.

Torment clawed at me the entire night but finally I realized that this was one woman's opinion, and even though it may not have been a great painting, I was determined to see what creativity God could unleash in me. I chose to overcome the disgrace of that circumstance. I went back for the remainder of that week to see if God could turn my pain into something beautiful. He did. I ended up with several great paintings that hung over our fireplace for many years. My choice to not accept shame brought incredible joy, confidence and, ultimately, radiance into my character.

2. Removing Sinful Shame (Real Shame)

This shame is the result of real guilt that eats away at us, causes us to lose sleep, makes us physically sick, destroys relationships and perpetuates excessive brooding.

David encountered this type of guilt from his sin, "The pressure never let up; all the juices of my life dried up. Then I let it all out; I said, 'I'll make a clean breast of my failures to God.' Suddenly the pressure was gone—my guilt dissolved, my sin disappeared" (Psalm 32:3-5, MSG).

There is incredible freedom when we make a "clean breast" of our guilt that is caused by sin. Forgiveness is a sign of real love. In the same way that Jesus died for our sins, we are commanded to die to the sins others do to us.

Let's remember some fundamentals of forgiveness:

1. It's hard.
2. Don't deny your feelings of bitterness, powerlessness and vengefulness.
3. Understand that forgiveness is not forgetting or condoning. We have been injured and we have to acknowledge what we felt was unjust and wrong.
4. Look at your own imperfections, judgments and be frank about your part in the event.
5. Put yourself in the other's person's shoes—it will give a clearer perspective of what happened.
6. Persevere—it will take time. Much longer than you think.

Gabrielle Bauer, who wrote the article "To Forgive: Divine" says, "Even when you want to forgive, it can seem impossible. That's why it takes time, patience, insight and grace to grow past a hurt and go on with your life."[80]

It will take time, but one day we will be able to say like David did: "Praise the Lord, O my soul, and forget not all his benefits—who forgives all your sins and heals all your diseases, who redeems your life from the pit and crowns you with love and compassion"(Psalm 103:2-4, NIV).

Unusual Treasures, Unusual Radiance

When we ask God to help us choose to clean the dirt from our lives, we will find treasures of radiance in the most unusual places. My girlfriend Sherry has a story that is a great analogy for that exact statement. While she was on her vacation to the Cayman Islands she decided to do the usual touristy adventure of snorkeling. She tells it this way, "As I was coming up to the shore I came face to face with a huge rock. I put my hand on the rock to steady myself, and I felt something. I picked up an object that looked like a dirty, cheap, costume jewelry ring." She then tells how she tucked it away and almost forgot about it until one day she saw a jewelry store and thought, "Hey, just for the fun of it I will have it appraised." They cleaned the dirt from the ring and appraised it as a 1.75-karat diamond worth over twenty thousand dollars. Each time I see her, I like to pick up her left hand and examine this glittering, amazing, huge diamond ring. It was originally seen as a worthless, slimy chunk of dirt, but when it was cleaned off it displayed its original beauty. In fact it is gorgeous and radiant beyond anything I have seen in a long time.

In the same way, you and I can experience unusual beauty when we make a deliberate choice to give God permission to help us clean the dirt from our lives to expose our hidden radiance.

I feel confident in telling you this because I know you are one of God's magnificent creations. You are radiant beyond your wildest comprehension. Please choose to believe it. It will empower you to make choices that will radically change the path of your life's journey. Making choices from a shame-based identity keeps us from accepting God's goodness in our lives. Instead of allowing shame to fuel your choices, deliberately make confident, good choices based on knowing God's unconditional love for you.

Remember that you are a child of God; you have been forgiven and you are a winner.

Choices That Enrich Your Life

1. When someone criticizes you, choose to believe that it is not a personal attack.

2. When you have a compulsion to help others out of a need to give yourself value, choose to do it from a good and pure motive.

3. When you feel angry, choose to go back to the wound that caused the anger and then see if your anger is due to your shame.

4. When a family member reminds you of a past sin, choose to respond out of a heart that has been forgiven. Then be courageous enough to confront that person in love and tell them, "God and I have dealt with the past, and from now on can we please leave this topic out of our conversation?"

5. When you don't finish a project perfectly, choose to measure yourself in light of what God can do through you, not what other people will think about you.

6. When you feel overwhelmed, irritated and resentful, choose to see this as a wound of trying to live your life to please other people instead of God. Instead, ask God to help you restore your health and joy by helping you find the root of your people pleasing.

7. When you feel arrogant, choose to see this as a coverup for feeling worthless.

8. If you are afraid of intimate relationships, choose to let God heal your past hurts of feeling unloved and abandoned. Learn to trust again one step at a time.

9. If you feel stupid and worthless, remind yourself that you are God's workmanship—a masterpiece (Eph. 2:10, NIV).

10. If you feel like you are an alien in this world, choose to believe that you are not an accident; but in fact, you were chosen before the foundations of the earth were formed (Eph. 1:3, NIV).

11. When you feel like nobody likes you, choose to initiate an honest, loving relationship with someone with likeminded values.

12. When you feel like an inadequate Christian, choose to believe that "He who began a good work in you will carry it on to completion until the day of Christ Jesus" (Phil. 1:6, NIV).

13. When you are ready to make another decision that will help you to simply survive, choose to go out of your comfort zone and make a decision that will help you thrive.

14. When you feel worthless when someone points out an error or a fault, choose to remember that you have value because you are a child of Creator God.

15. When you feel ashamed for any reason, choose to remember that you have the power to surrender or forgive, depending on which shame you are dealing with. Then do it!

Stop and Ask God To Help You Change Sand to Pearls

Begin by asking: God, what am I ashamed of?

S Scripture: "I sought the Lord, and he answered me; he delivered me from all fears. Those who look to him are radiant; their faces are never covered with shame" (Psalm 34:4-5, NIV).

T Thanksgiving: God, I can hardly believe that You can take away all my shame. I do know that when Moses had an encounter with You, his face became radiant. Thank You that You can also make mine radiant.

O Observation: This Bible verse tells me that I have to make an intentional effort to seek You so that You can deliver me from my fears and shame. I realize that I have a lot of shame in my life, and I need Your help in surrendering shame and dealing with guilt from sins that have not been dealt with. You are the only one who can help me, because You are the only one who knows what is in my heart.

P Prayer: God, please help me to open my secret box to see if there is any hidden shame tucked away in there. I ask You to help me on this journey of identifying my shame so that I can come to You to help me remove it. God, show me and help me discover the wounds that have caused me to limp through life, not being all that You have created me to be. God, in which area of my life am I simply surviving, and not thriving in the way You intended me to live?

Thank You that You scorned shame for me—that You looked it right in the eye and refused to accept it. Teach me to deal with shame in the same way, to see it for the ugliness that it is and the horrible power it has over my life. Help me to run to You and Your unconditional love so that I will have the fortitude and determination to deal with it and remove it from my life. Make me aware and quicken my heart when shame causes me to make unwise decisions. I pray with all my heart that I will make choices that will determine a pathway of living the life You intended for me to live. Help me not to dwell on the things of the past that have robbed me of joy, but to look forward to the hope I have in living a life free of shame. Thank you.

Amen.

Chapter 12

Panic or Prayer

God, Stop the Wind

When a Christian shuns fellowship with other Christians,
the devil smiles. When he stops studying the Bible, the devil laughs.
When he stops praying, the devil shouts for joy.

—CORRIE TEN BOOM

*M*atthew kept stopping, looking up at the sky and saying, "Stop it, stop it." My three-year-old grandson seemed agitated while we were on our ritual walk to the mailbox. I finally asked him, "Matthew, who are you talking to?" He said, "Nana, I'm talking to God; I want Him to stop the wind." I smiled and said, "Oh," and kept walking. Matthew lives in southern Alberta, Canada, where the wind is so strong that often it stopped him from being able to play outside. He was tired of the wind robbing him of his fun; and he wanted it to stop—now.

As soon as we arrived home, he jumped on the sofa and stood there looking out the window at the sky. Soon I heard the excited shout, "Nana, look! God stopped the wind!"

I love his simple, trusting faith, talking to God like He was his best friend. I desire that we all have this kind of faith in prayer, never doubting or being critical, but trusting God like a little child. Children have not yet learned to be cynical or doubtful. They love and trust unconditionally. That is why Jesus tells us to become like little children. "At that time Jesus, full of joy through the Holy Spirit, said, "I praise you, Father, Lord of heaven and earth, because you have hidden these things from the wise and learned, and revealed them to little children. Yes, Father, for this was your good pleasure" (Luke 10:21, NIV).

Over the last fifteen years I have probably read over 100 books on prayer, trying to understand the power and beauty of this supernatural form of communication. I conclude that reading and studying prayer will not, in themselves, reveal its mystery. There is no formula, method or twelve-step program that will give us the results and answers we look for. We must become as trusting children and begin to *experience* it.

I have been involved in our church as a prayer director, teacher or mentor for fifteen years. People often ask me, "Heidi, why are you so passionate about prayer?" I always answer the same thing: "I experienced its power in a season of desperation."

When I first became a Christian I prayed all those nice, structured, predictable prayers. They were patterned prayers uttered out of obligation rather than passion, and I had little faith that God would really answer me. On a Sunday in 1994, in a divine encounter in my walk-in closet, God turned my perception of prayer upside down.

My husband Dick had died playing basketball on the evening of Thursday, December 8, 1994. Over the next three days my darling children, my sister and friends stayed with me in my home, comforted me, fed me, cried with me and took me to church that following Sunday. During those days I tried to pray; but my heart was in so much pain, and I had such a hard time breathing that all I could mutter was, "Peace, God, please give me peace." Sitting in church the following Sunday without my husband at my side evoked emotions I was not prepared for. I was in excruciating pain, hyperventilating and waiting for the church service and the agony to come to an end. When we arrived home I bolted upstairs to my bedroom to find some privacy and to change my clothes. As I stepped into the walk-in closet, out of the corner of my right eye I could see one of my husband's shirtsleeves sticking out. This was the last shirt he had worn and he had hastily put it away; consequently the sleeve still hung out. My eyes were glued to that sleeve; it tormented me. All of a sudden the realization hit me; he was never coming home again. I sunk down onto the carpeted floor in the closet and started to sob and shake violently as though my whole body was being ripped apart. Anger rose up in me and between sobs I confronted God, "So where are you now, God? You said You would never leave me or forsake me, but I can't find any peace. I need to know that You are right here or I won't be able to survive. Where are You God? Where are You?" Almost instantly warmth flooded through me from the top of my head to the tip of my toes, and a peace saturated my whole body in a way I had never experienced before. My heart stopped its frantic pounding, my sobbing was finished, and I sunk to the floor, calm, warm and peaceful. At that moment I was confident that God had heard my cries of anguish. He was right there in that closet, and I knew He would be with me throughout the rest of my life. In my searing moment of desperation I found my greatest revelation. I knew that God had seen my sobbing and heard my shouting. He answered my prayer. Like a child, I began to believe in the unexplainable, supernatural power of prayer.

One of our greatest human needs is to be heard. When we know we are heard we feel understood and wonderful transformation begin to happen. A relationship with God is no different. Before we can have a fervent, passionate prayer connection with God we need to know that He is listening to every word like our best, trusted friend. This chapter is not going to be about a lot of doctrine and theology about prayer. Simply being smarter and having more head knowledge about prayer probably won't start you on the path to a fervent prayer life. This chapter is to spur you on so that you will become so passionate about prayer that you will choose to pray instead of panic.

If we aren't captivated by God, prayer is nothing more than gutting it out, a tedious task, another obligation we should fulfill. We check it off as another item on our to do list. It's like the cod liver oil that my mother

made me take daily when I was little, because it was *good for me.* Which
describes your attitude towards prayer?

- Prayer is like writing thank you notes. It's a nice thing to do, but
  another obligation I need to fulfill.
- Prayer is like my marriage; it can be rewarding but it is hard work. I
  don't want to add more work to my daily commitments.
- I want to like praying, but I don't understand it, so I don't do it.
- Why bother? God doesn't answer prayer anyway.
- I really want to start praying, but don't know how.
- I enjoy my prayer time, but would like to go deeper.

I want to make you passionate about starting or strengthening your
prayer life by asking you to believe God like a little child, trusting that He
will stop the wind.

Listen

Would you agree that when we are in a loving, intimate relationship with
someone, we build intentional times in our schedules to talk to each other,
listen, share stories, laugh and share each other's hopes, dreams and disappointments? That is exactly what we need to do with our Heavenly Father.
We need to "Be still, and know that I am God" (Psalm 46:10, NIV). We
cannot know God in the noise, confusion and clamor of our tightly packed
schedules that leave little margin for solitude. In order to know who God
is, we must slip into a quiet place so that our minds can shift focus from
our circumstances, delight in His beautiful character and be open to receive
what He wishes to reveal to us. The Greek word for "know" is *ginosko*. It
is an intensely powerful word which directs us to such intimacy as "sexual
intercourse between a man and a woman".[81] We can only find such profound closeness when we are committed to nurturing and experiencing that
kind of relationship.

Brad Jersak in his book *Can You Hear Me?* explains this intimacy in a
fresh way: "I believe Jesus is saying to you today, 'I am your friend. I am not

your psychic hotline. I'm not interested in impressing you or making you impressive to others. I want intimacy. So before you rush ahead and ask me to lay out the future of the world for you, would you be willing to be my friend for a while?'"[82]

Most of our prayer lives consist of hurried, short staccato sentences thrown up to heaven as we dash out the door and head into our stop-and-go traffic. We desperately hope that we will quickly hear from God, so that we can solve this problem and move on to the next item on our overcrowded task list. It's hard for us to deal with, but there is no other way to hear from God except in the silence.

The prophet Elijah was fatigued and discouraged, and feeling a little sorry for himself after two of his great spiritual victories. He went into the desert, sat under a broom tree and said to God, "I have had enough Lord…. Take my life" (1 Kings 19:4, NIV). He was all alone and he desperately needed to hear from God.

> Then he was told, "Go, stand on the mountain at attention before God. God will pass by." A hurricane wind ripped through the mountains and shattered the rocks before God, but God wasn't to be found in the wind; after the wind an earthquake, but God wasn't in the earthquake; and after the earthquake fire, but God wasn't in the fire; and after the fire a gentle and quiet whisper. When Elijah heard the quiet voice, he muffled his face with his great cloak, went to the mouth of the cave, and stood there. A quiet voice asked, "So Elijah, now tell me, what are you doing here?" (1 Kings 19:11-14, MSG).

I get goose bumps when I read this. I am sure that most of us have felt like Elijah, alone, depressed and desperately needing affirmation and answers from God. Sitting under our own broom trees or in a closet we want to shout, "God, are You really out there?" God revealed Himself in a *quiet whisper* to Elijah, and God will reveal Himself to you in your silence. You will be able to hear Him when He whispers to your heart, "Now tell me, what are you doing here"?

Look Up

Many times when I lead prayer teams, I have everyone take a couple of deep breaths so that we can quiet our hearts, wash away toxic stress, and begin to focus on God and all He is to us. When we purposefully take our eyes off our circumstances and look into the eyes of our trusted friend, we will find new hope. Debbie Williams in her book *Pray with Purpose, Live with Passion,* says we are to "look up and praise." While several Hebrew words describe praise, the one most frequently used is the verb *halal,* from which we get the word "hallelujah." This primitive root word means to "shine, to flash forth light, boast."[83] When we take time to praise our God, we will open our hearts to receive God's healing, powerful, restoring, transforming light. I have learned from Debbie Williams the powerful exercise of doing the A-Zs of God. I ask people to add their own descriptions as we go along, but this is how we might start:

Abba Father
Beloved Savior
Comforter
Door
Eternal
Forgiver
Gardener
Helper in Times of Trouble
Immanuel
Just
King of Glory
Light of the World
Mighty Rock

Never Give Up on Us
Our Dwelling Place
Protector
Quickening Spirit
Refuge
Shepherd and Shield
Tower of Strength
Uplifter
Vine
Wonderful
eXalted
Yahweh
Zealous

Now that we are sitting down with our faithful friend, and focusing on Him, we need to know that He is listening and aware of our words. He assures us over and over again: "When I was desperate, I called out, and God got me out of a tight spot" (Psalm 34:6, MSG). "Praise be to the Lord, for he has heard my cry for mercy" (Psalm 28:6, NIV).

God continues to assure us that He is very close and that He always hears us. He is our rescuer and will always throw us a lifeline that is uniquely made for the struggle or situation we're in.

Remarkable Secrets

The deeper we get to know who God is, the more we will crave spending time with Him. There is so much He wants to reveal to us: "Ask me and I will tell you remarkable secrets you do not know about things to come" (Jer. 33:3, NLT).

God waits to reveal the answers to life's questions. Frequently we look for answers in textbooks, seminars, workshops and the musings of our friends. These are all wonderful sources, but why would we think we can find life's answers anywhere besides God, the One who knows every hair on our head, and knew every one of our days even before we were created in our mother's womb?

I was on a lunch date with my husband when we looked over to another table and saw two friends sitting with food in front of them, each of them texting. They were together, but not looking at each other or speaking; each was totally immersed in a piece of technology made of plastic and metal. This took priority over their relationship. It made me so sad to watch this, but that is how many people interact these days. We don't take the time to listen to each other's hearts or see the pain or joy in each other's eyes. If we can't make the effort to listen to each other when we are sitting across from one another, how will we make time for God, who is invisible and seems so far away? If we are waiting for something supernatural to come along and help us with our toils and trouble, we simply have to make that intentional time with the One who reveals all the secrets of heaven and earth.

Griping, Panicking, and Asking

Now that God has your focused attention, and you know He is listening, He is waiting for you to tell Him everything that is troubling you. He knows you and I carry heavy burdens every day. When our loved ones, our children, grandchildren or other people we love walk around with frowns on their faces, their shoulders hunched over and look like they are carrying the weight of the world on their shoulders, we want to help them, but they need to ask. Peter the fisherman wrote to us saying, "Cast all your anxiety on him [God] because he cares for you" (1 Peter 5:7, NIV).

Do you have a boatload of trouble?

- God designed marriage; so He cares deeply when your marriage is in trouble.
- He cares when you are overwhelmed. You may have gotten yourself into this tight agenda, but He is willing to help you untangle this mess.
- When your bank is account is empty and the cupboards are bare, God wants to provide.

- You are in the middle of relationship conflict. God is the healer of broken hearts and the restorer and reconciler of relationships.
- You have never been able to deal with your abortion, sexual abuse or sexual sin. God will heal and restore your heart.

Why are we afraid to ask? Are we afraid of losing heart if God does not meet our expectations? Or are we afraid we will make God look bad if He doesn't answer the way we need Him to?

In their practical, insightful book, *God Will Make a Way*, Dr. Henry Cloud and Dr. John Townsend give this encouragement: "The very great news is that when we ask God for help, we have instantly transcended our own limitations. We have stepped over to the side of a God who has infinite ways to grace us with all the resources we really need."[84]

God has all the resources to bring us through our battles. Sometimes, though, He may not change the circumstances; He may simply want to change our hearts.

Heart Change: Prayer or Panic

1. Griping

The first part of a heart change is to be gut level honest with God with all of our struggles. I call it being "naked and unashamed" the same way that Adam and Eve were in the Garden of Eden while they were still in beautiful, fulfilling harmony with God.

I love King David's honesty in the Psalms; lamenting, cursing, telling God to kill his enemies, then praising God and extolling him with words of admiration and begging for forgiveness. When we are going through our own meltdowns, our minds can be a mass of confusion, and sometimes bad thoughts form in our minds. David was not afraid to express his emotions, and neither should you or I be. God knows what's in our hearts, so let's be true to ourselves and tell God everything—every nasty detail—and then ask for forgiveness. If we keep silent and ignore our sins, we will become physically sick. "When I kept silent, my bones wasted away through my groaning all day long" (Psalm 32:3, NIV). But David also knew the power of forgiveness from his loving God when he said, "You are forgiving and good, O Lord, abounding in love to all who call to you" (Psalm 86:5, NIV).

While griping doesn't sound very spiritual, when we share our deepest frustrations, disappointments and yearnings with the One who truly loves us and listens to our cries, we will feel validated and be able to move forward.

2. Stop Panicking

The second part of our heart change is to trust God and pray before we panic. King David should have talked to God about his restlessness and boredom before he was tempted and had an affair with Bathsheba. After he slept with this beautiful woman, instead of panicking and having her husband killed, he should have come clean with God and asked for help. Even though David had a deeply intimate relationship with God, this time he knew he had really messed up and he panicked.

It is a scientific truth that "nature abhors a vacuum"; unfilled spaces are unnatural.[85] When you are physically hungry and go grocery shopping, have you noticed how just about everything looks so tempting you can hardly wait to sink your teeth into it? You probably end up buying more groceries than you planned because everything is so inviting and looks so delicious.

The same principal applies to our spiritual life. When we are walking around with an empty heart, we are a walking, talking minefield. An empty soul is a danger just waiting to happen because we will do whatever it takes to fill that empty heart.

King David tempted that very fate when he decided to stay home and not do what he was supposed to do; go with his men to fight on the battlefield. By staying behind, I surmise that he was probably bored, his soul was empty and he needed to fill it. Yet again, God's unconditional love and compassion overwhelm me when he told David: "I gave you your master's house and his wives and the kingdoms of Israel and Judah. And if that had not been enough, I would have given you much, much more" (2 Sam. 12:8, NLT). God knows all our struggles and weaknesses, and He longs for us to share those with Him. He might be whispering to you right now, "Are you feeling lonely, empty or sad? Do you feel like you have been overlooked? Is everyone and everything turning against you? Is life not turning out the way you thought it would? Talk to Me and tell Me everything. I am listening and I want to fill your empty heart and give you even more than you imagined."

Nothing is too hard for God. Before we run off and have an affair, or do something that will hurt us and cause pain for many people, He wants us to come to Him and tell Him what that emptiness is in our hearts. He can help; we just need to ask.

3. Start Asking

The third part of our heart change takes place when we finally ask. Even though this should be our first step, oftentimes it is our last desperate recourse. Think of all the anguish, sleepless nights, text messages to friends and valuable time and energy we could save if we run to God first.

Remember He is your one true trusted friend who is passionate about helping you. His promise is: "And I will do whatever you ask in my name, so that the Son may bring glory to the Father. You may ask me for anything in my name, and I will do it" (John 14:13-14, NIV).

What we ask in Jesus' name must be completely in character with what Jesus would do if He were walking in our shoes, living our lives, going where we go and meeting with those we meet. To be "in His name" is to have our identity so buried in His that we are totally and completely covered in Christ. To any observer in the heavenly realm we are operating as if Christ himself were acting or speaking.

Even though it doesn't seem like it, Jesus does hear and answers every one of our prayers. We love it when He says "yes"; we don't like it when we have to "wait"; and often we think that our prayers have simply not been heard and answered. I believe they actually have, but it might have been a "no." It is hard for us to receive the "no" when we have prayed for a loved one to be healed, a marriage restored, a child's addiction broken, or a much needed job obtained. On this side of heaven we will most likely never understand the nos or the long silences; but our God who made the mountains and oceans is much wiser than you and me. One day we will understand.

It is hard for us to speak into a vast, endless space that contains millions of stars and planets, and where we seem as insignificant as the tip of a pin. But God reminds us that He knows our name, and that He knows everything about us. "Lift your eyes and look to the heavens: Who created all these? He who brings out the starry host one by one, and calls them each by name. Because of his great power and mighty strength, not one of them is missing" (Isa 40:26, NIV).

God is very close to us; He is probably with you right now as you are reading this. He knows your name and everything you are going through this very moment. Talk to Him; tell Him whatever is on your heart.

4. Not Like Yadda Yadda

The fourth heart change takes place when we release our prayer from our heart into God's outstretched, waiting hand. The Hebrew word for "hand" is *yad*, "the *open* one, indicating power; in distinction from, the *closed* one."[86] For me this is an incredibly beautiful and powerful concept of me handing over my worries and concerns, and placing them into an *open hand* of someone who sincerely wants to help me. It's the same relief I get when I have an overwhelming load of work and screaming deadlines, and a friend reaches out their open hand and says, "Come on, hand it over to me; I'll do it for you." God promises us that He will orchestrate everything in our lives in His perfect timing—not too early, and never too late. "For the revelation awaits an appointed time; it speaks of the end and will not prove false. Though it linger, wait for it; it will certainly come and will not delay" (Hab. 2:3, NIV).

Prayer is not empty words that sound like "yadda, yadda," which is meaningless blabber. Every one of our words are heard by an infinite God who is standing and waiting with open hands, ready to help.

As I was growing up, each night I heard my mother's prayers on the other side of her bedroom door. I know she never stopped praying all the years that I chose to do life my way, stubbornly rebelling against our family values and God. I know that her prayers broke through the darkness and pain in my heart, and took me to the foot of the cross where I found my personal, intimate relationship with God.

My mother is now eighty-five, and as all our bodies do as we get older, she is growing fragile and her health is starting to fail. While I was writing this chapter, I spent a night with her, just to watch over her in case she had a dizzy spell. As I heard the familiar, steady words of my dear mother, talking to God about everything in her life, I sat on the other side of the wall and wept. She took everything that was in her hand and left it in the *open hands* of her God, the One whom she trusts for every aspect of her life. She tells us over and over again that God is her everything; her provider, peace, joy, comforter, shelter in times of trouble and her friend. My mother has modeled for me that peace and hope come through the power of praying instead of panicking.

Prayer is the innocent, sweet words of a three-year-old child asking God to stop the wind, and the whispered, broken words of someone ready to go to their homeland. God hears every word in between and is waiting with open hands and open arms.

Choices That Enrich Your Life

1. You would like to start praying but you don't think you can "do it right." Choose to believe that prayer is talking to God, not some foreign dialogue with fancy words. Start talking to Him today.

2. If God is not answering your prayer about your circumstances, choose to believe that at the present moment, He is more interested in changing your heart.

3. You find it hard to love some of the people in your family, neighborhood, ones you may be working with, or even people at your church. Choose to pray for them and ask God to help you love them.

4. You think prayer is useless. You tried it a few times and it did nothing. Choose to believe that we need to be persistent and wait for the

answer. The Bible tells us, "The earnest prayer of a righteous person has great power and produces wonderful results" (James 5:16, NLT).

5. You worry a great deal about everything and you just can't seem to stop. Choose to believe that God wants us to be anxious for nothing, and He does not want us to live in fear. He tells us, "Don't worry about anything; instead, pray about everything. Tell God what you need, and thank him for all he has done. Then you will experience God's peace, which exceeds anything we can understand" (Phil. 4:6-7, NLT). Choose to believe that as you keep praying, peace will come.

6. You have prayed for years that your husband and children will experience a personal relationship with Jesus; but nothing is changing. Choose to believe that God knows what's going on. Keep praying and never give up.

7. You have been unemployed for a long time and you feel that you have been abandoned by everyone, including God. Choose to believe that God never abandons us, that He knows your name, and that your prayers will open a door for you. Keep looking and asking for a miracle for God to open the right doors.

8. Someone you love is dying and you are praying for their healing, and nothing is happening. Choose to believe that the God who created such a magnificent human being has an appointment for them that they are not going to miss. Choose to believe that their ultimate healing is in God's hands.

9. Your life feels out of control. Go into your closet, close the door, and talk to God about it. God is a God of order and not confusion; choose to believe that ultimately through your prayers and diligence in listening to God, He will help you learn to live the kind of life that is full of abundance.

10. Your prayer life is not all that you want it to be: you want more. Choose to make intentional time, even if you have to mark it in your calendar, away from noise and clutter, so that you start being "still and knowing God."

11. Your prayer life seems as dull as a relationship that has no passion or hope for a better day. I want to ask you, what does your God look like? Choose to believe that when you see God as your trusted friend, He will become captivating and your prayers will become intimate conversations.

12. You're afraid to spill your anger when you talk to God. Guess what? He already knows the words in your mind and heart. Choose to believe that when you tell God just how you feel, it will clear the clutter out of your heart.

13. You simply cannot find quiet time to spend with God. Choose to believe you can't afford not to find time with God.

14. Is there a right or wrong way to pray to God? I ask you, is there a right or wrong way to speak to other people? Choose to believe our relationship with God is much like our relationship with other people, only better.

Stop and Ask God To Help You Change Sand to Pearls

Begin by asking: God, how can I cultivate a powerful prayer life?

S   Scripture: "Ask me and I will tell you remarkable secrets you
do not know about things to come" (Jer. 33:3, NLT).

T   Thanksgiving: Thank You, God, that You love me enough
that You want me to talk to You. It is absolutely amazing to
me that You want to tell me the secrets about who You are
and about the way You made me. Thank You that You hold
the future in Your *open hands* and that I can trust You to take
care of my cares and worries.

O   Observation: God is not as loud as an earthquake, or as visible as a blazing fire. I realize that in order to find God I
need to become silent. Everything seems to work against me
to find the silence I need to cultivate a captivating, intimate
relationship with God. I know that I need to make a deliberate choice to stop and pray.

P   Prayer: You are God Almighty, my beloved Savior, You have
been my Comforter and You are always there waiting for
me with open hands and open arms. God, I ask that You
would take these powerful truths from my head knowledge
and sink them into the very depth of my soul so that I can
begin to experience Your great love for me. I stand in awe
and amazement that You, the Creator of all the stars, planets
and meteors, want to share Your secrets with me. God, I am
open and willing to sit with You and listen to what You want
to speak into my heart. I ask, in the name of Jesus, that You
would help me to orchestrate my priorities so that I have You
first on my mind when I wake in the morning. Help me to

be deliberate about setting aside time with You so that I can pour my heart out to You and share my life with You. Teach me how to listen, and how to know when I am hearing Your voice, not the voice of my own selfish desires or the voice of an imposter. Help me fall in love with You, so that You are the only one I trust with my life. Thank You for loving me enough to never let me go.

Amen.

Chapter 13

Career or Calling

You Are Standing on Holy Ground

*Here is the test to find whether your
mission on Earth is finished: If you're alive, it isn't.*

—RICHARD BACH

More than once I have said to my colleagues, "Working in a car dealership is better than watching reality TV, sitcoms or soap operas. Not many people would believe the drama and excitement we experience here daily." They always nod and smile in agreement.

In August 2009 I celebrated my fifteenth year being a controller in a car dealership. I am now passionate about my career and all the people I work with, but it hasn't always been that way. When I began my spiritual journey in 1978, I had the impression that anyone who was on a fervent passionate spiritual journey to make a difference in this world needed to go on a mission trip to Africa. Today I would drop everything to go there, but back then it left my stomach in knots just to think about it.

In those years I was an administrator in a law firm, and secretly hoped that someday God would reveal His calling for my life and supernaturally airlift me out of there to do something more important. I kept praying and asking Him to help me make an eternal impact on this world. He answered in the strangest way; He put me in a car dealership. It made no sense, and occasionally I got frustrated and felt useless, just biding my time until something better came along. My mind compartmentalized my life into two worlds, the sacred and the worldly. The sacred place is where I wanted to be in, on full-time service to God, going out into the world teaching the word of God, saving lives, feeding the hungry and loving the poor. The worldly arena is where I was stuck; and I saw it as a temporary holding pattern and obstacle until God pulled me out of there to do something more valuable for His Kingdom.

I encounter a lot of people who come into the dealership and I noticed something that greatly disturbed me; a *collision of values*. I saw too many "Sacred Sunday Christians." When I came across them in church on Sundays they were smiling from ear to ear, carrying a big fat Bible; but when I saw them at my workplace they were different. I wished they would be friendly and smile. It hurt me to watch them being rude, demanding, obnoxious and cheap, squeezing every last nickel out of every sale. One day, God showed me I was no different. I was on the telephone with a very demanding woman and felt extremely annoyed and started to be rude to her. After all, she couldn't see me, and would really never know who I was. The next moment was a divine encounter that completely shattered my perception of my compartmentalized values. God whispered to me, "Heidi, careful, you are standing on holy ground!" I almost dropped the phone like a hot potato and immediately the tone in my voice changed. That divine nudge challenged me to see wherever I am, or whatever I do, I am representing God as a child of the King and I am standing on holy ground. I have underlined the verse in my Bible that reminds me continually: "Whatever you do, work at it with all your heart, as working for the Lord, not for men" (Col. 3:23, NIV).

"Whatever I Do"

That verse has revolutionized my way of thinking and living. My whole attitude changed toward my job, my recreational activities, my marriage, family, church—everything. I had to understand that God's essence is love, and that our mission here on earth, as His children, is to saturate *everything we do* with love and grace. As humans it is hard to understand that love is the bottom line of everything we do and say, because we have been taught to think differently. It is much easier to put things into compartments; this is right and this is wrong, this is successful and this not. This includes everything you and I are doing at this moment. I believe one of the most undervalued yet worthy "whatevers" is a mother at home raising children. I see her as a vessel of God nurturing, guiding and shaping little children's souls with godly values. There are so many other "whatevers" that we don't realize we have the power and ability to impact the world. Our holy ground can be working as a:

- Parent. This is probably one of the hardest places to love completely, and yet it is where most of our nurturing and teaching comes from.
- Check-out Clerk. This gives you endless opportunities to smile and encourage frazzled people all day long.
- Receptionist. This is a very challenging and demanding position where the tone of your voice and your responses impact people in ways you may never know.
- Manager. Here you have the prospect of influencing people's lives in ways that can impact their careers paths, their values and standards for integrity.
- The list is endless. You may be retired, a volunteer, a service technician, a telemarketer, a computer technician, an accountant, or lawyer, "whatever" you do.

If you profess to be a Christ-follower and want to impact the world with God's love, each of the places where you are presently standing become holy ground.

Tim Schroeder in his book *Life by the Hour* says, "It's a heresy that suggests life can be divided into neat compartments. Most often they are labeled, 'Sacred' and 'Secular,' and behind those labels many put the *'good'* and *'bad.'* Instead of learning to live well and honor God with ALL life, with our WHOLE being, instead of serving Him in 'whatever we do,' we've convinced ourselves that God really only cares about one compartment, so we can slack off in the others."[87]

That was my way of thinking; that my career was simply a transition period until something more meaningful, life-impacting, came along.

I confess that I am fascinated with some of the reality TV shows where there is the ultimate winner of some great prize, or a large amount of money. I watched *Runway Canada* for a season and it was almost agonizing for me to watch each week as someone was eliminated from the show. The final words were, "You're out, because you do not measure up." Those are harsh words, but we can identify with them because in this competitive, callous world we live in, when we don't succeed at what we have been called to do "we're out, because we have not measured up."

When we have a personal relationship with God we are always secure in His love and forgiveness for our sins, and we're never out because we didn't measure up. This is the vision through which we need to see and treat people wherever we are. Frankly, the workplace has become my biggest training ground and most challenging mission field, because this is where I am learning how to love and accept people just the way they are. I can't label people, either. I like this person because they go to church, show compassion to the homeless people and have a generous spirit. Or, I don't like this employee because he swears, is selfish and is rude and difficult to get along with. My workplace has been my boot camp to learn to love and accept everyone the same way that Jesus does.

When Jesus encountered a despised Samaritan woman coming to a well to draw water, He shattered all boundaries. Jews and Samaritans were not to associate with each other. Not only was this woman a Samaritan, but she also had been married five times and was now living with a sixth man. Double jeopardy. Jesus did not despise or condemn her; instead He offered her hope by telling her about *living water* that would satisfy her soul's desires. Our physical bodies hunger for food and water, but we forget that our spiritual souls also need to be filled. God is spirit, and when we enter into an intimate personal relationship with Him, He fills our soul with living *water*, which is the word of God that will satiate our thirsty souls.

I have worked with people who have been divorced three or four times, are living with a lover, or are having affairs. It is not my job to pigeonhole them, feel self-righteous and despise them. My challenge is to offer them some living water.

"Work At It With All Your Heart"

1. Heart Shaping

It startled me to learn that Jesus is more interested in shaping my character than my career. When we die, we really don't take anything else with us but that which emerges out of our character. God is in the business of shaping our hearts, and it is through people who rub us the wrong way. Let's face it, some people can bring out the worst in us, but that is exactly what God wants to work on. This is how He does it: "God knew what he was doing from the very beginning. He decided from the outset to shape the lives of those who love him along the same lines as the life of his son" (Rom. 8:29, MSG).

So God knew what He was doing when He put me in a car dealership to shape me into His image. At times it has been a painful process because I've learned some startling truths about myself.

2. Heart Over Pebbles and Rocks

There is a story about a man that ran across the U.S.A. from coast to coast. After he arrived at his destination, there were TV cameras and journalists just aching to hear his remarkable story. So they asked him questions about the dangers and toughest parts of his amazing accomplishment.

> "Was it the scorching sun or the dark cold nights?"
> "No," said the man.
> "Was it the fatigue, the aches in your body and the lack of sleep?"
> "No," said the man.

"Was it the loneliness, the endless stretch or highways or the horrific winds?"

"No," said the man.

"Well, what was the hardest part in finishing this achievement?"

He replied, *"It was the sand in my shoes."*

This is a story I can relate to. I know about the daily frustrations and irritations that gnaw away at us until we are limping around feeling angry and defeated. But it is those tiny constant annoyances that are the methods God uses to shape us and rub our rough edges off. It is exactly those people who are tough to get along with that are the ones chipping away at us to make us more like pearls. Kerry and Chris Shook explain it this way: "Finally He likes to use people in our lives to enrich our character, to chip away at our selfish edges that prevent us from loving others the way Christ does. Each one of us has people in our lives that are hard to love."[88]

Some days it feels like all the different personality types are not just pebbles in our shoes, but we are actually throwing rocks at each other. In this greatest tension lies our most powerful opportunity to display the most beautiful and powerful love. Again, I want to respond like Jesus did when he was confronted by the self-righteous Pharisees about a woman who had been caught in adultery. They wanted to throw stones at her but Jesus responded: "All right, but let the one who has never sinned throw the first stone!" (John 8:8, NLT). Jesus' answer grips me because when we are in a "holy" place, we need to respond like Jesus did; instead of throwing rocks we have to stop and love and accept each person the way that Jesus modeled for us.

I had a Pharisee encounter a couple of years ago where someone confronted me with blame, judgment and anger, throwing verbal rocks at me. I should have known better because I thought I had learned how to deal with different personalities. On this particular day I just wanted to throw rocks right back at this person—and I did. Afterwards I felt horrible and I couldn't wait for the next day to come so that I could apologize. My apology mended our differences, but it taught me another huge lesson, again. My workplace is holy ground and I must learn to respond in love. This may be the only time I have the opportunity to show sacrificial love to this person—and that needs to be my mission. In every work environment we will encounter those heated, confrontational situations where differences need to be worked out. There is a healthy, constructive way to do this—and it is certainly not by throwing rocks.

3. Heart Over Process

I have been in management for over twenty-five years and have struggled with the tension of showing grace and love to people, yet being a diligent manager and following company policies. Our teaching pastor in my present church, Pastor Tim Schroeder, gave a message one Sunday that impacted me profoundly and has become my grid for managing people. He said we must always choose "people over process."

It doesn't matter where you are right now, in your workplace with a demanding, high-profile career, in your home, church, working on a computer or selling furniture; look around you. Everything you see will one day be gone except the breath of God that is within every person you meet. I have to keep telling myself that ultimately this is the only thing that matters. No matter how thorny or complicated my challenge is on any given day, I must remember that it is people that matter to God.

"As Working For The Lord, Not Men"

I have discovered that spreading the good news of Jesus Christ by going on a mission trip is actually easier that being on mission in my workplace. When I went to Poland during the summer of 2009 to speak about spiritual transformation, the people there were ready, with hearts open to learn and receive. In our worldly workplaces, people's hearts are often closed up tight and they don't want to know anything about God. But, there are practical, everyday practices that we can apply that will stand out from the norm.

1. Honesty

We have read enough disturbing headlines it the last number of years to know that we live in a world that strives for success through lies, deceit and manipulation. Simply telling the truth in our "whatever" places will show people that our prosperity does not come from material possessions, but from "knowing God's favor, anointing and power that is working in our lives to fulfill his purposes." [89] It is also vitally important that we let our yes be yes and our no be no, and that we are responsible and follow through on our commitments.

2. Don't Gossip

Gossip is a weapon of mass destruction in any workplace and I simply will not do it. By setting the example of not talking about people, I set myself apart as being visibly different. It also causes people to feel safe with me and trust me. Refusing to talk disparagingly behind people's backs will make all of us beautifully different.

3. Tangible Evidence of Appreciation

After interviewing people and conducting performance evaluations for all these years, I have found that the number one factor for employees to function at their best in their work environment is to *feel appreciated*. This is a huge deal for people and I try to show my appreciation to my staff by occasionally bringing flowers or candies, taking them out for special meals or bringing something back for them when I come back from a trip. It doesn't take much to make people feel appreciated; we just need to make a point of doing it.

4. Be an Example

Something as simple as coming to work on time, not abusing cell phone privileges during work hours and not taking advantage of longer lunch hours or coffee breaks will make you stand out from the crowd.

5. Sweat the Small Stuff

When I arrive at the dealership in the morning, I try to go around and say "good morning" to see how people are doing. I can see it in their eyes when they are sick and need to go home; when they are stressed and overwhelmed, we need to listen to them and find ways to make their load lighter. When they are facing difficult situations in their families, we need to be able to step into their shoes to see their struggle from their perspective and assist them in whatever way we can. Don't be afraid to tell people you will pray for them; it may sound strange to them but they will appreciate it.

6. Treat Everyone as God's Creations

Even when people treat us badly, we must treat them with love and respect. This is hard to do but the long-term results will amaze us if we persevere.

God has promised you and I that when we spread His word, it will bear fruit and accomplish His Kingdom purposes. "As the rain and the snow come down from heaven, and do not return to it without watering the earth and making it bud and flourish, so that it yields seed for the sower and bread for the eater, so is my word that goes out from my mouth: It will not return to me empty, but will accomplish what I desire and achieve the purpose for which I sent it" (Isa. 55:10-11, NIV). I believe that with all my heart because I see the concept of seed yielding food at work in the world around me.

My son-in-law Tim runs a huge farm near Grassy Lake, Alberta, Canada, and I have watched him sow canola seeds and I have seen the growth of the plants. That seed did not grow raspberries or barley; it grew what was planted—canola.

I have great comfort and peace in believing God's promise that when I model Christ and speak His truths, it will bear fruit. We may not see the growth immediately; maybe somebody else has to come along and water and fertilize it, but it will bear some fruit. I have seen evidence of this over the years in surprising and reassuring ways. One day as I was sitting in my office working, I looked up and saw one of my employees hovering in the doorway. She had an intent look on her face and said, "Heidi, can I come in and talk to you and ask you how we get to heaven?"

I have to remind myself that we are all spiritual beings walking around in human bodies and we will all someday leave this earth. No amount of money or striving will give me the complete satisfaction I am looking for. The way God shapes my own character, and uses me to impact other people's character is the only thing that will ultimately matter.

Calling

There are indeed people who have had a distinct calling on their lives to do something specific for God. We must remember, however, that we cannot put a method or formula to hearing from God. We probably would all like the clarity of the experience that Moses had in the desert when God talked to him from a burning bush; but God speaks to our unique personalities in different ways. Dan L. Hays, a fellow writer from Forth Worth, Texas, puts it this way: "When I was six years old, I knew I was supposed to be a writer. It was not something anyone ever said to me; I knew it was something of God. It's not like I heard God speak, it was just a calm, inner knowing that I first became aware of when I was six. There was a certainty about that direction that has never wavered."[90]

I never heard God's voice in a specific way; He orchestrated my life completely differently. He was preparing me to work on "holy" ground while I was on "worldly" ground. Looking back I see that first of all God had to shape my character to prepare me to be a speaker and author. He had to smooth out a few self-righteous, critical edges so that I could be authentic and be able to speak to people in all walks of life. This process did not happen overnight: it took many years for God to prepare my character, unleash the gifts and abilities to prepare me for what I do today. I am so blessed to be able to do both. I am passionate about being a controller in a car dealership, *and* teaching and speaking to women across Canada, in the United States and even in Europe. I have learned to do "whatever I do; do it for the Lord with all my heart."

God has placed gifts in all of us that can be used to leave our fingerprint on this earth. Marcus Buckingham has done extensive research on helping people finding their strengths so that they find their best role in life. In his book *Finding your Strongest Life*, he guides the reader to discover the role they were born to play. He says, "It's easy to slip into a role we assume is right for us.... Base your decision on the fact that you value yourself enough to be inquisitive, to ask questions, and to listen closely to what your emotions are telling you. Only then will you find the moments that strengthen you. Only then will you discover the role you were born to play."[91]

If you are stuck in a profession that leaves you joyless and unfulfilled, it is time to look at your one and only life. Your life is too valuable to go through the drudgery of just putting in time until something better comes along. Choose to think outside of your normal routine, look backwards and see what you loved to do when you were a little child. God has placed something beautiful and unique inside of you; you need to be intentional in partnering with God to discover it.

The happiest, most confident women I know are those that have faith in what they do—a faith that comes from using the gifts that our Creator God has given us. Each one of us has an exceptional, purposeful calling, to be the very best that God created us to be.

It's Never Too Late

In the fall of 2009, my daughter Michelle and I were walking out of our church after seeing and hearing a presentation about Africa. We were both silent as we reflected on what we had just heard. We had listened to the plights of Africa: of the millions of children that had no parents, or young women sold into slavery, and the lack of water and education. We were both wiping away tears when I said, "Honey, when your children get a little older, why don't we as a family go to Africa and do something that makes a difference in their lives?" She replied, "Mom, I am so into that!"

It's never too late, and who knows, maybe I will get to go to Africa. But now I am passionately ready to do the "whatever" God prepared me to do, wherever I am.

Choices That Enrich Your Life

1. If you are unemployed right now and you just can't find any work, choose to believe that God has something for you to do and it will unfold in time. Choose to keep believing day after day even when you don't feel like it.

2. Are you in a job that is drudgery, seems meaningless, and you feel that your life has no purpose? Choose to be bold to search for your strengths and find a profession that fits you. Quiet your mind, pray and ask God to help you receive emotional signals from your spirit that will help you identify when you are on the right track; then start searching out something that is uniquely suited for you.

3. Do people in your workplace annoy and frustrate you? Choose to believe that God uses these people to bring out the worst in us so that we can become who we were actually created to be.

4. You are a "stay at home mom" with daily, repetitive jobs that make you feel like you are never accomplishing anything or making any difference in this world. Choose to believe that if you are caring for your children and family, you are making the most dramatic impact possible on people's lives.

5. Are you retired and tired of always "doing"? Choose to believe that our role on earth is never done until we take our last breath. One way to bring incredible hope and change into this world is to pray; and we can all do that.

6. Are you an ordained pastor or someone trained to be in full-time church ministry? If this is a frustrating, painful or empty time for you, choose to believe that this may be a time of rest or change, and that leaving your full-time ministry does not make you a lesser person.

7. Are you in the process of graduating from school and everyone keeps asking you, "So what are you going to do when you graduate?" Choose to believe that you do not have to have one concrete answer, but that you may have to try a few different avenues before you find your unique niche in this world.

8. Have you gone to school and are qualified for a particular occupation but you can't find a job in that field? Choose to believe there is something out there for you but that you have to be diligent about finding it. Choose to do something valuable in your "waiting period" and see every day as a gift to make a difference in someone's life.

9. Do you believe your life's desires line up with a "calling" on your life for full-time ministry, but nothing is opening up for you? Choose to believe you are in full-time ministry every morning your feet hit the floor.

10. Do you give your workplace the best each day but you constantly feel overworked and overlooked? You are not getting that raise you think you deserve and people treat you with less respect than you deserve? Choose to look inside yourself first. Are you giving other people the respect and work results they deserve? If so, then ask God for boldness to reveal a time and place that you can talk to your superiors about a well-deserved raise.

11. You are sure you have a calling to be a speaker but there are no opportunities for you to utilize this gift. Choose to pray that God will open doors for you. If this is a calling on your life, God will open doors for you at the right time.

12. If you think you are a workaholic and just can't make yourself stop, choose to look inside and see what is making you so driven. I think we have all discovered by now that money never buys our happiness. I have never sat by anyone's bed that was dying who said, "I wish I had worked more." Choose to bring priorities into line.

13. I'm fifty-five and I don't know what I want to be when I grow up. You may have been going through life sabotaging your dreams and desires for other people, or may have never found your niche. Choose to believe it is never too late to find something you are passionate about. Ask God what that something is.

14. You retired early and are still young, and your days are filled with golfing and meaningless stuff. Choose to believe that we are never

really fulfilled until we are doing something to make a difference in this world.

Stop and Ask God To Help You Change Sand to Pearls

Begin by Asking: God, am I throwing stones at anyone?

S Scripture: "All right, but let the one who has never sinned throw the first stone!" (John 8:7, NLT).

T Thanksgiving: God, I am so thankful that You never throw stones at me when I do things that hurt people. Thank You that You came to earth to show us how to love each other, no matter who we are, what we do, or where we work.

O Observation: Some sins are big, and some of them small; but we all sin. It's so much easier to point to someone else doing something bad and judge them for it. We spend most of our hours at our workplaces where we see a lot of people's sins; so that is where we have to be careful that we don't throw stones.

P Prayer: Thank You, God, for Your living word, which continues to breathe life into me and teaches me how to love. Thank You that You came to earth and walked amongst us to teach us how to treat each other wherever we are so that we can live in harmony and unity. I am so grateful that You give us occupations that fulfill us, earn us some money, but most importantly give us opportunities to spread Your love and grace. Forgive me for the times I have felt self-righteous and thrown stones.

God, make me a dispenser of Your love wherever I go and whatever I do, so that when I leave people will be able to say, "There goes a reflection of God's love." Help me to know that I am on Your mission field as soon as my feet hit the ground in the morning, and wherever I go. Help me also to see each person I encounter as Your beautiful creation, to treat them with respect and strive for them to be all that You created them to be. Help me to discover each day what gifts You want to unleash in me to bring glory and beauty into Your Kingdom. God, You are incredibly loving and kind, and I thank You for loving me so unconditionally. Amen.

*A*ll the choices that I have talked about in this book have the ability to transform your one and only beautiful life. Choosing to grit your teeth and doing ten or twelve steps to success is not what this is about. We can all try harder to be nice, less busy, focus on relationships or be less judgmental and critical; however, the first crisis that we encounter will probably push our default button and transform us back to our old, predictable self.

This is not about learning how to act differently; we need God's power to completely transform our minds. This is what the Bible says, "Don't copy the behavior and customs of this world, but let God transform you into a new person by changing the way you think. Then you will learn to know God's will for you, which is good and pleasing and perfect" (Rom. 12:2, NLT).

Wouldn't you want to know God's perfect will for your life? There are two prayers that start us on a gorgeous, transformed life, changing us from the inside out.

1. The first prayer is to have Jesus, the Son of God, forgive us from all our past sins. All the bad things we have done in our life have a lot of power over us, but when we confess these sins to God, He forgives each and every one of them. The Bible promises us, "But if we confess our sins to him, he can be depended on to forgive us and to cleanse us from every wrong" (1 John 1:9, TLB). We can then begin to live a new life out of a cleansed heart and begin our lifelong journey of becoming more magnificent and free each day.

1.

   Pray this simple prayer with me:

   Lord Jesus, please come into my life and be my Savior and Lord.
   I acknowledge that I have sinned, and I ask You to please forgive me

for my sins. Please fill me with the Holy Spirit and give me the gift of eternal life. Start me on the road to living the glorious life that You have created me for. Be my power by giving me the mind of Christ to help me make wise, life-transforming choices so that I can know Your good, pleasing and perfect will for my life.

Thank You that You will. Amen.

2. Now that God has forgiven all of our sins, we need to turn around and forgive everyone that has hurt us. This is not just a nice gesture; the Bible commands us to forgive. "Be gentle and ready to forgive; never hold grudges. Remember, the Lord forgave you, so you must forgive others" (Col. 3:13, TLB).

   I can tell you with all sincerity that forgiving everyone in my life that wounded me has been the most powerful, freeing choice I have ever made. I urge you; do not let another day go by without choosing to forgive everyone in your life that has caused you pain, disappointment, resentment, anger or rejection. Letting go of this pain is not about letting them off the hook and setting them free; it is about Jesus setting you free. One of the human qualities that makes people more like Jesus is the divine act of forgiveness. There is nothing easy about forgiveness; it will probably be the hardest choice you will ever make in your life, but I guarantee you that it will be most freeing, joyful transformation you will ever experience.

When I walk people through the steps to forgiveness, I use the following thirteen steps. In order to do a complete, supernatural heart work, I suggest that you go through all of them with each person on your list.

   1. Write on a sheet of paper the names of the persons who offended you.
   2. Face the hurt and the hate. Write down how you feel about these people and their offenses.
   3. Acknowledge that Jesus died for your sins.
   4. Decide you will bear the burden of each person's sin. All true forgiveness is substitutionary, as Christ's forgiveness of us was.

5. Decide to forgive. Forgiveness is a conscious choice to let the other person off the hook and free you from the past. The feelings of freedom will eventually follow.

6. Take your list to God and pray the following: "God, I choose to forgive (name) for (list of offenses—what they did-how they made you feel)."

7. Destroy the list. You are now free.

8. Do not expect that your decision to forgive will result in major changes in the other person.

9. Try to understand the people you have forgiven. They are victims also.

10. Expect positive results of forgiveness in yourself. In time you will be able to think about the people who have offended you without hurt, anger or resentment.

11. Thank God for the lessons you have learned and for setting you free.

12. Be sure to accept your part of the blame for the offenses you suffered.

13. Do something to bless the person who has hurt you.

Forgiveness is hard and the feelings of freedom may take longer to come than you think. Please persevere. If someone has hurt you deeply, it may take many prayers until the ugly, painful hook is completely released from your heart. One day you will be able to look that person in the eye and bless them. Then you will know you have experienced the powerful transformation from illusions of struggling to create your ideal life, to living the joy and freedom of the life that you know you were created to live. It's time to take the grit out of your shoes and dance with freedom and joy.

Endnotes

1   Marcus Buckingham, *Find Your Strongest Life: What the Happiest and Most Successful Women Do Differently* (Nashville, TN: Thomas Nelson, 2009), 90-91.

2   http://thesaurus.reference.com/browse/intimidate, (November 2009).

3   Used by permission from Beth Hanishewski of Mindset Coaching, The Inspired Habits Coach.

4   Marcus Buckingham, *Find Your Strongest Life: What the Happiest and Most Successful Women Do Differently* (Nashville, TN: Thomas Nelson, 2009), 14.

5   Kerry & Chris Shook, *One Month to Live: Thirty Days to a No-Regrets Life* (Colorado Springs, CO: Waterbook Press, A division of Random House Inc., 2008), 26-27.

6   John Bevere, *Breaking Intimidation: How To Overcome Fear and Release the Gifts of God in Your Life* (Lake Mary, FL: Creation House, Strang Communications Company, 1995), 98.

7   Used by permission from Beth Hanishewski of Mindsets Coaching, The Inspired Habits Coach.

8   John Maxwell, *Dare to Dream...Then Do It* (Nashville, TN: J. Countryman, a division of Thomas Nelson, Inc., 2006), 69.

9   Liz Curtis Higgs, *Embrace Grace* (Colorado Springs, CO: WaterBrook Press, 2006), 118-119.

10 W. Phillip Keller, *Joshua: Man of Fearless Faith* (Waco, TX: Word Books, 1983), 41.

11 Priscilla Shirer, *One in a Million* (Nashville, TN: LifeWay Press, 2009), 132.

12 http://en.wikipedia.org/wiki/Sound_barrier (October 23, 2009).

13 Liz Curtis Higgs, *Embrace Grace* (Colorado Springs, CO: WaterBrook Press, 2006), 121.

14 http://www.livingwithanxiety.com/a-feel-good-natural-cure-for-anxiety-stress-depression.htm/, *Ladies Home Journal*, (August, 2006).

15   Daniel Goleman, *Social Intelligence: The Revolutionary New Science of Human Relationships* (New York, NY: Bantam Dell, A Division of Random House, 2007), 228.

16   http://en.wikipedia.org/wiki/Friends (September 7, 2009).

17   Dr. Jan Yager, Ph.D., *Friendshifts* (Stamford, CT: Hannacroix Creek Books, Inc., 1st Edition, 1997, 2nd edition and cover photograph 1999), 106.

18   http://www.blueletterbible.org/lang/lexicon/lexicon.cfm?strongs=G430 (September 30, 2009).

19   Rosemary Flaaten, *A Woman and Her Relationships* (Kansas City, KS: Beacon Hill Press of Kansas City, 2007), 106.

20   Tom Rath, *Vital Friends* (New York, NY: Gallup Press, 2006), 36.

21   Used with permission from Lesley-Anne Evans.

22   Used with permission from Lesley-Anne Evans.

23   Dr. Jan Yager, Ph.D., *Friendshifts* (Stamford, CT: Hannacroix Creek Books, Inc., 1st Edition, 1997, 2nd edition and cover photograph 1999), 230.

24   *Vine's Expository Dictionary of New Testament Words* (Iowa Falls, IA: Riverside Book and Bible House), 13.

25   Used by permission from Cheryl Klippenstein.

26   "Naked and not ashamed" is a phrase used by Joseph R. Myers, in *The Search to Belong* (Grand Rapids, MI: Zondervan, 2003), 67.

27   Kerry & Christ Shook, *One Month to Live: Thirty Days to A No-Regrets Life* (Colorado Springs, CO: Waterbrook Press, 2008), 100.

28   http://www.imdb.com/title/tt0758758/ (November 13, 2009).

29   http://movies.coolnsmart.com/into-the-wild-quotes-2007/ (November 13, 2009).

30   The Random House College Dictionary, Revised Edition, 1975.

31   Carol Kent, *Tame Your Fears and Transform Them into Faith, Confidence, and Action* (Colorado Springs, CO: NavPress, 2003), 113.

32   Lynne Hybels, *Nice Girls Don't Change The World* (Grand Rapids, MI: Zondervan, 2005), 54-55.

33   http://preachingtoday.com/sermons/article_print.htlm?id=47346 (August 5, 2008).

34   Dr. Henry Cloud, *9 Things you Simply Must Do To Succeed in Love and Life* (Nashville, TN: Integrity Publishers, 2004), 181.

35   Warren W. Wiersbe, *The Best of A.W. Tozer: 52 Favorite Chapters* (Harrisburg, PA: Christian Publications Inc., 1978), 122.

36   Bob and Audrey Meisner, *Marriage Undercover* (Huntsville, AL: Milestone International Publishers, 2005), 152.

37   Gary Thomas, *Sacred Influence* (Grand Rapids, MI: Zondervan , 2006), 26-27.

38   Ibid., 71.

39   Shaunti Feldhan, *The Bible Study, For Women Only* (Nashville, TN: LifeWay Press, 2006), 10.

40   Ibid., 15.

41   Gary Thomas, *Sacred Influence* (Grand Rapids, MI: Zondervan , 2006), 55.

42   Bob and Audrey Meisner, *Marriage Undercover* (Huntsville, AL: Milestone International Publishers, 2005), 149.

43   Laura Petherbridge, *When "I Do" Becomes "I Don't"* (Paris, Ontario, Canada: David C. Cook Distribution Canada, 2008), 237.

44   Rick Warren, *The Purpose-Driven Life: What on Earth Am I Here For?* (Grand Rapids, MI: Zondervan 2002), 64.

45   Daniel Goleman, *Social Intelligence: The Revolutionary New Science of Human Relationships* (New York, NY: Bantam Dell, A Division of Random House, Inc. 2006), 66.

46   Ibid., 164.

47   Dr. Archibald D. Hart, *Thrilled to Death, (How the Endless Pursuit of Pleasure is Leaving Us Numb)* (Nashville, TN: Thomas Nelson 2007), 11.

48   Ibid., 2-3.

49   Ibid., 83.

50   Rick Warren, *The Purpose-Driven Life*, (dailydevotionals@purposedrivenlife .com) *Margin or Marginless?*, January 5, 2009.

51   Dr. Archibald D. Hart, Ibid., 11.

52   Ibid., 23.

53   Used by permission from Cheryl Klippenstein.

54   Rick Warren, *The Purpose-Driven Life: What on Earth Am I Here For?* (Grand Rapids, MI: Zondervan, 2002), 252.

55   Dallas Willard, *Renovation Of The Heart* (Colorado Springs, CO: NavPress 2002), 118.

56   *Vines Expository Dictionary of New Testament Words* (Iowa Falls, IA: Riverside Book and Bible House), 1133.

57   Andy Stanley, *The Best of Catalyst: 2007, Leadership from the Inside Out,* Message #4, October 9, 2007.

58   The Random House College Dictionary, Revised Edition, 1975.

59   *Vines Expository Dictionary of New Testament Words* (Iowa Falls, IA: Riverside Book and Bible House), 460.

60   The Phobia List, http://phobialist.com/, (November, 2009).

61   H. Norman Wright, *Freedom From The Grip of Fear: A Process of Reclaiming Your Life* (Grand Rapids, MI: Fleming H. Revell, A Division of Baker Book House Co., 2003), 24.

62   David Foster, *The Power to Prevail, Turning your Adversities into Advantages* (New York, NY: Warner Books Inc., 2003), 64.

63   Carl Kent, *Tame Your Fears and Transform Them into Faith, Confidence, And Action* (Colorado Springs, CO: NavPress, Bringing Truth to Life 2003), 201.

64   David Foster, *The Power to Prevail: Turning your Adversities into Advantages* (New York, NY: Warner Books Inc., 2003), 63.

65   Harriet Lerner, Ph.D., *The Dance of Fear: Rising Above Anxiety, Fear, and Shame to Be Your Best and Bravest Self* (New York, NY: HarperCollins Publishers Inc., 2004), 208.

66   Lisa Beamer with Ken Abraham, *Let's Roll* (Wheaton, IL: Tyndale House, 2002), 307-8.

67   Grace Fox, *Moving from Fear to Freedom* (Eugene, OR: Harvest House Publishers, 2007), 222.

68   Gordon MacDonald, *A Resilient Life* (Nashville, TN: Thomas Nelson, 2004), 98.

69   *Vines Expository Dictionary of New Testament Words* (Iowa Falls, IA: Riverside Book and Bible House).

70   *Vines Expository Dictionary of New Testament Words* (Iowa Falls, IA: Riverside Book and Bible House).

71   Kerry & Chris Shook, *One Month to Live: Thirty Days To A No-Regrets Life* (Colorado Springs, CO: Waterbrook Press, 2008), 147.

72   Nancie Carmichael, *Surviving One Bad Year: 7 Spiritual Strategies To Lead You to a New Beginning* (New York, NY: Howard Books, 2009), 160.

73   Dr. Henry Malone, *Shame: Identity Thief* (Irving, TX: Vision Life Publications, 2006), 13.

74   John Ortberg, *Christianity Today,* http://www.christianitytoday.com/leaders/newsleter/2008/cln80609.html, June 10, 2008.

75   James Strong, *Strong's Exhaustive Concordance of the Bible* (McLean, VA: MacDonald Publishing Company).

76 The Random House College Dictionary, The Unabridged Edition (New York, NY: Random House, 1975).

77 Harriet Lerner, *The Dance of Fear* (New York, NY: HarperCollins Publishers), 220.

78 The Random House College Dictionary, The Unabridged Edition (New York, NY: Random House, 1975).

79 Katie Brazelton, *Pathway to Purpose for Women* (Grand Rapids, MI: Zondervan), 173.

80 Gabrielle Bauer, "To Forgive: Divine," *Homemakers, Life & Times*, November 2005, 32.

81 http://www.blueletterbible.org/lang/lexicon/lexicon.cfm?Strongs=G1097&t=KJV (January 6, 2010).

82 Brad Jersak, *Can You Hear Me?* (Abbotsford, British Columbia, Canada: Fresh Wind Press, 2003), 62.

83 Debbie Williams, *Pray with Purpose, Live with Passion* (West Monroe, LA: Howard Publishing Co. Inc., 2006), 20.

84 Dr. Henry Cloud and Dr. John Townsend, *God Will Make A Way* (Brentwood, TN: Integrity Publishers, 2002), 21.

85 http://www.howstuffworks.com/question200.htm, (December 10, 2009).

86 James Strong, *Strong's Exhaustive Concordance of the Bible* (McLean, VA: MacDonald Publishing Company).

87 Tim Schroeder, *Life by the Hour* (Victoria, British Columbia, Canada: Trafford Publishing, 2009), 156.

88 Kerry and Chris Shook, *One Month To Live, Thirty Days to a No-Regrets Life* (Colorado Springs, CO: Waterbrook Press, 2008), 1909.

89 Bob Meisner, *Your Dream Is Your Future,* It's a New Day Ministries, (Winnipeg, Manitoba, 2009), November 2009 newsletter.

90 Used by permission from Dan Hays, Fort Worth, Texas, http://www.DanLHays.com.

91 Marcus Buckingham, *Find Your Strongest Life* (Nashville, TN: Thomas Nelson, 2009), 98.

Also by Heidi McLaughlin ...

The secret desire of every woman is to be more beautiful both inside and out, and yet we can't seem to find the magic formula. We are bombarded with solutions, but nothing seems to satiate our longing for value and significance. The fact is that we are beautiful because we are created in the image of God, who is the essence of beauty. It's all right there inside of us—we just need to allow God to reveal it to us and unleash it. Find out how in *Beauty Unleashed*.

Available from Heidi McLaughlin (www.heartconnection.ca), Christian bookstores, Amazon.ca or Barnes & Noble.

Study Guide also available—contact Heidi via www.heartconnection.ca.

Heidi McLaughlin also speaks at women's conferences, retreats and special events across Canada and internationally. Her powerful, life-changing messages draw women into a place of intimate connection with each other and with God. Her messages are rich with humour, passion and truth, and liberally sprinkled with personal stories. For more information, visit her website at www.heartconnection.ca.